POINT A TO POINT B

THE LIFE AND TIMES OF AN ACCIDENTAL UBER
DRIVER IN CALIFORNIA'S WINE COUNTRY

JAMES MACFARLANE

Point A to Point B

The Life and Times of an Accidental Uber Driver in California's Wine
Country

An Odyssey

A Memoir

An Askew Glance at the Human Condition

By James Macfarlane

ISBN: 978-0-692-95035-7

Library of Congress Number: 2017914752

Contact: uberjames@uberjames.com

To Johnny and Jessie. Thanks for befriending me.
You greased the wheels and thus made the adventure
much more fun.

To my "test readers" and typo detectors
Cathy, Jessie M., Gail, Katy, and Wade

To each and every person who took a ride
in the Prius Super-Duper Uber car

CONTENTS

DETAILED CONTENTS

PREFACE

The Tale of the Blind Men and the Elephant

Once upon a time there lived six blind men in a village. One day the villagers told them, "Hey, there is an elephant in the village today." The blind men had no idea what an elephant was. They decided, "Even though we would not be able to see it, let us go and feel it anyway." All of them went to where the elephant was. Every blind man touched the elephant.

"Hey, the elephant is a pillar," said the first man who touched the leg.

"Oh, no! It is like a rope," said the second man who touched the tail.

"Oh, no! It is like a thick branch of a tree," said the third man who touched the trunk of the elephant.

"It is like a big hand fan," said the fourth man who touched the ear of the elephant.

"It is like a huge wall," said the fifth man who touched the belly of the elephant.

"It is like a solid pipe," said the sixth man who touched the tusk of the elephant.

The blind men began to argue about the elephant and every one of them insisted that he was right. It looked like they were getting agitated. A wise man was passing by and he saw this. He stopped and asked them, *"What is the matter?"* They said, *"We cannot agree on what the elephant is like."* Each blind man told the wise man what he thought the elephant was like. The wise man calmly explained to them, "*All of you are right. The reason every one of you is telling it differently is because each one of you touched a different part of the elephant. So, actually the ` elephant has all those features that you all said.*"

"*Oh!*" the blind men said in unison. There was no more fight. They felt happy that they were each right.

Very few people can see the "whole elephant" of life. We all have our own view of things based upon what we've experienced. We often think that someone with a different point of view is wrong and that we are right. Yet right and wrong are often a matter of perspective, which may be altered when one sees the bigger picture. The author was constantly reminded of this story while driving for Uber.

It's the same old story we've heard time and again. Man with hyper sensitivity to smoke is forced from his California home due to a nearby forest fire. Man's twenty-three year old car dies while on the road. Man buys new car. New fires breaking out around the state chase man -and man's new car- out of multiple safe havens. Man nearly goes insane watching TV in motel rooms whilst roaming the land... then finds solace as an Uber driver.

Oh, you didn't hear that one? Well this book tells that story. The fire was in Big Sur, California, world renowned vacation destination of three million visitors each year. The Big Sur fire lasted three months and was classified as the most expensive in US history. As the summer unfolded additional fires broke out across the state, and as luck would have it, each new fire happened to ignite near the man's latest sanctuary. For a while the man, that's me, your author, was dodging fires like raindrops.

Evacuated from the homes of relatives and friends, and falling between the cracks of various emergency support systems such as the Red Cross, I had to fashion a way survive on the road and pay for the growing pile of travel expenses. When my old but reliable car unexpectedly died I found myself in a new car and shortly afterward spawned the idea of putting the car to work driving for Uber.

Ride sharing is one of many disruptive technologies spreading across the world like wildfire. With miniaturization and ubiquitous smartphone cameras everyone can now be a photographer.

With blogging technology everyone can now be a writer and opinion maker. And with mobile computing, GPS, and mapping software everyone can now be a part of the rideshare industry. We can be taxi drivers.

Driving for Uber was a singular experience. Although the work in my view is a job, not a career, in that context it was the most fun *job* ever. I met people from virtually all walks of life, and rendered and received lessons in psychology, sociology, and anger management. I maneuvered and was outmaneuvered, had a pile of interesting and surprising experiences, and there was even an "Imperial entanglement" (a brush with the cops).

The whole experience reinforced a notion impressed upon me years ago when reading an obscure book titled 'Growth of the Soil'. The underlying message in that book was: *We are all living the same lives.* This theme emerged again and again as your author got a glimpse into the lives of singles, couples, and families as their lives unfolded before and during their Uber ride.

Virtually everyone who took a ride wanted to hear of my saga. Unlike a taxicab ride, people getting in an Uber car, at least where I was driving, insisted on gaining familiarity with their driver. And many of those inquisitive passengers wanted to hear an *Uber story* as well. It is these two elements, combined with the venue of driving in a popular wine tasting region that prompted this book.

While driving for Uber I was exposed to every cabbie cliché in the book. I got a *"Step on it!"*, a *"Keep the meter running"*, a *"Follow that car"*, and even a *"Home James."* And was all the happier for it.

Hope you enjoy this book.

ONE
THE EXODUS

How it all Began

"There is nothing so stable as change"
- Bob Dylan

How it all Began

The year was 2016. The month was July. The event was the most expensive forest fire in US history. This was the so-called 'Soberanes' fire, ignited by an illegal campfire in the place I call home, Big Sur, California. Big Sur is an unspoiled wonderland, a world-wide vacation destination for those seeking pristine coastal beauty. It's where the Santa Lucia Mountains plunge steeply into the Pacific Ocean, and a drive up the adjacent State Route 1 reveals a nearly identical view as was seen by travelers decades ago.

If someone had mentioned in June that the following month would find me evacuated from my home, chased around central California by no less than four fires, that I would buy a new car (which I never do), and become a full-time driver for Uber Technologies Inc., I would have responded.... "Uh huh."

Yet that was precisely what unfolded. On August 3rd, 12 days into the fire, I threw some belongings into my 1993 Toyota Corolla station wagon and steered the car toward parts unknown.

My house was not under immediate threat from the nearly uncontained fire. Our tiny community was not in the path of the firestorm on that day. Rather, the clear and present danger was to my lungs, which are hyper-allergic to smoke. I was born with a less-than-perfect respiratory system and over the years have become increasingly intolerant to any airborne pollutant. After nearly two weeks of barely getting by with a 3M N95 filter mask and a hepa air purifier running at full tilt 24/7, the realization came that the exodus I'd been dreading was at hand.

The unique thing about the Big Sur lifestyle for many is that once you get ensconced into the rhythm of that unplugged existence you tend to not want to step away from it. Even to go to town for groceries. Over time I and many of my neighbors have reduced the frequency of town runs to once or twice a month. So getting me out of Big Sur would take something like an act of congress. Or in this case a mindless, rationalized act of someone who had deluded themselves into thinking they could build a bonfire in a restricted area of the woods and not have it get out of hand. Someone once said that human beings are not rational, but rather, they *rationalize*. That is a difficult assertion to argue with.

TWO
TO YOSEMITE AND BEYOND

Exit Stage Right

*"It's a dangerous business, Frodo, going out your door. You step
onto the road, and if you don't keep your feet, there's no knowing
where you might be swept off to"*
-Bilbo Baggins

Exit Stage Right

Once in the car I turned the key and made the first navigational
decision. The easy one. There is only one main road running
through Big Sur; California State Highway 1, which parallels
the Pacific Ocean. To the north brewed the Soberanes fire, so I
pointed the automobile to the south and the next chapter of my
life began to unfold.

The consensus among the various voices in my head was to
head up to Yosemite. One of the most serene and beautiful
spots on the planet. This whole *-presumably short-* fire thing
was a great excuse for a little vacation. Right? Yosemite, lying to
the east across the expanse of the San Joaquin Valley with its
5,000 foot elevation, would surely provide a sublime shelter
from the firestorm taking place along the coast.

The trick was how to get there. The smoke from the fire had
spread well to the south and east. I really should have abandoned the effort at that point and headed to an airport, as California was fast becoming untenable for a lunger like myself.
The restraining factor was that although I am 90% retired from
a career in IT, I have two clients in Big Sur to serve. One is a
local K-12 school. The school year would be starting in a few
weeks and invariably there would be some network related
startup pains to deal with. There was also an Inn that needed to
keep its Wi-Fi system, room booking software, and the all-

important point-of-sale system running. I couldn't in good conscience walk (or fly) away from that.

So with a mask firmly affixed, the station wagon blasted across the valley at near warp speed and climbed up to Yosemite via Hwy 41. Indeed, the smoke had found its way into every nook and cranny along the route. It had blanketed the towns along the Hwy 41 corridor leading eastward to State Route 101. Further to the east the smoke had settled into the foothills bracketing Interstate 5. Same with the paralleling State Route 99 to the east. Only after ascending Hwy 41 from the floor of the central valley toward the Sierra foothills did the smoke abate. The haze steadily cleared until at the 1,000 ft marker the standard issue, semi-clean California oxygen circulated in my lungs. Phew.

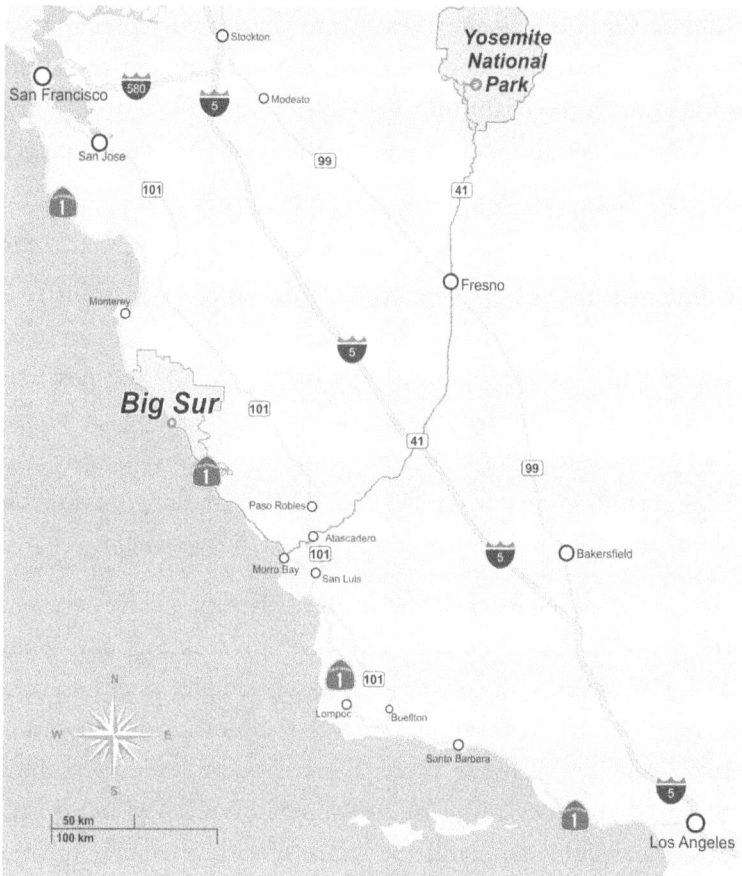

Big Sur to Yosemite

Yosemite Paradise

Yosemite Valley was as it always is; peaceful... breathtaking... and full of summertime tourists. In fact there were more cars in the Park than I'd ever seen. A line of cars was backed up a mile or two where Hwy 41 enters the valley and the road runs parallel to the Merced River. There are two lanes for inbound traffic, but in recent years one lane has been dedicated exclusively to tour buses (and cop cars). Inevitably, and possibly due to poor signage, passenger cars were occasionally popping out of the car lane and zooming down the bus lane. So you could either watch the beautiful river rush by on the left, or turn and watch all the cheaters fly by while the rest of the crowd played stop-and-go.

The lesson there was that regardless of how well the US economy is doing in general, the California tourism industry is nearly overheating. My home town of Big Sur has an even worse traffic problem from the influx of tourists the past few years. Some say it is without precedent. There are places on the highway where traffic slows to a crawl as vehicles navigate past the protruding cars of foreign visitors parked along unparkable shoulders, with wheels overlapping onto the pavement.

Anyway, I never reached the front of the line giving access to the populated area of the valley. While stopping and going along the river road I started checking lodging prices and got scared off. Life in Yosemite could be wonderful for a month or two... kicking it in the tent cabins of Camp Curry or high Stylin' it at the extravagant Ahwahnee Hotel. My credit card however would not stand the strain of either habitat. In high season even the lower end motels outside the valley were extracting $250 plus a night from one's wallet. It was starting to look like the Soberanes fire was not going to be extinguished anytime soon so I started looking for a longish term solution. I had relatives in Santa Barbara, but there were no spare bedrooms and I was concerned about wearing out my welcome on a multi-month stay. What to do? What to do...

THREE
A CALL FOR HELP

Exploring the Options
A New Hope
You're Right Where You Need to Be

"Curiouser and curiouser!"
- Lewis Carroll

Exploring the Options

After crossing the Merced at a convenient bridge somewhere shy of Yosemite Valley proper I reversed course back down Hwy 41, and an hour or so later hit the mountain crossroads town of Mariposa. Accommodations here were more affordable than anything near Yosemite Park. Still, at $150 a night for the lowest priced motel in town, Mariposa was going to be only a temporary layover enroute to a more economical solution.

I started wondering if my situation qualified me for any kind of disaster aid, so I called the Red Cross. The well-known relief agency had set up an evacuation center just north of Big Sur for victims of the fire. Indeed, several mandatory evacuation orders were being issued as the fire encroached into populated areas. Interestingly, most evacuees had found solutions other than staying at the evac center, and at the time I phoned the facility had been shut down. The person on the other end of the toll-free national Red Cross phone number I had dialed referred me to the *local* Red Cross center. Following that lead I spoke with a kind-hearted gentleman who seemed to grasp my situation and assured me that although the evac center had been closed, he would work hard to find medium term housing for me. This was on a Friday. The man had promised to call the following Monday with an update. The conversation left me with a warm fuzzy feeling that help was on the way and that I needn't worry about exhausting my savings on motel rooms.

On Sunday I got a [premature] call from a local Red Cross woman. She was aware of my case and had called to give me an update. Surprisingly, the lady essentially countered everything the gentleman had stated earlier, and my warm fuzzies were extinguished faster than you can say wet noodle. I'll skip the details but the thrust of the conversation was that the Red Cross was not set up for longish-term solutions.

I should add that a suggestion was made by the Red Cross people to give **airbnb.com** a try. Airbnb, per their website, is *"... a trusted community marketplace for people to list, discover, and book unique accommodations around the world."* The impression had been given that Airbnb was donating accommodations to fire victims, but upon investigation it turned out that the organization was simply waving its booking fees, not the rental fee (thank you though!). Since Airbnb listings tend to be for higher-end niche properties, this was not an economical path to explore. Red Cross-wise, there were a couple of more conversations with the aforementioned kindly gentleman, but at the end of the day it was clear I was on my own.

A New Hope

Wait. It wasn't actually *the* end of the day quite yet. Somehow I had gotten plugged into a nationwide, privately held planning and relief organization called **recovers.org**. Recovers offers a pre and post disaster software based solution that matches private citizens capable of rendering some form of assistance with those needing that assistance. I spoke to a thoughtful woman named Sarah Blackstone who immediately used her resources to put out a call for the temporary housing situation I was seeking. The first thing Sarah did was to put me in touch with a representative of the Monterey County Association of Realtors, which was gifting displaced residents with $200 ATM cards. They sent me one of the cards, and although I never needed to tap it, the gesture was most kind. Then just a day or so later Sarah was back in touch with three housing candidates; a job with housing as a campground host in an area distanced from the ever-growing smoky patches around the state; a room in the house of a retired teaching couple; and an idea to approach Asilomar, a somewhat local 108 acre retreat and conference center bordering the Pacific Ocean, about an hour north of Big Sur. Good ideas!

The first solution, the campground host, was immediately disqualified however. I had done that type of work before and the demands of the job were a bit more than my generally weak health (in addition to the smoke allergy) was up for. I then spoke to the husband of the couple offering a room in his house and he was very welcoming. But what came through quite soon was that there was no way I wanted to impress myself on virtual strangers longer than a few days ... a week at most. It wouldn't be fair to either party. Again, thank you for the offer! But as more reports came in regarding the fire it was clear that this baby was going to burn for some time... perhaps even until Mother Nature doused it with rain (which in fact turned out to be the case). California was of course in a near record drought at the time.

The third item on the list hatched by my contact at Recovers was quite appealing. I could even trade Asilomar some IT services if they were interested. Sarah forwarded the synopsis of my situation as I had provided it to her (including a passage about being a middle-aged man, having no bad habits, quiet... so forth and such as). However, after a waiting period of several weeks the Asilomar staff informed Sarah they would not be able to make an accommodation available. So that was that.

You're Right Where You Need to Be

Not a problem. I felt no disappointment, let alone bitterness toward anyone, starting with the Red Cross and right down the line. My situation was putting me between the cracks of the support system. I also drew solace recalling some tight spots in the past where I'd been forced to work out the solution for myself. This is not a brag. It is a reflection on the notion that the universe tends to put us where we need to be at any given time. In this current crisis it was a matter of trusting that the circumstances required to push through this unfolding chapter of life would be provided. It was just a matter of being mindful and patient. These are two qualities I have in abundance.

Not.

But life had delivered a stream of lessons -severe at times-demonstrating that patience and mindfulness were qualities worth developing. So being dislodged from my very comfortable home was yet another chance to hone these disciplines.

I went into a holding pattern for a few days in Mariposa. Then a text came in from friends in Santa Barbara inviting me to weather the firestorm at their house. Nice! I accepted the offer. Beautiful Santa Barbara would not be a bad place to hunker down until the rain came. Not a bad place at all.

FOUR
A TWIST IN THE PLOT

Saying Goodbye to an Old Friend
Exodus Number Two

*"Life is what happens to you
while you're busy making other plans"*
- John Lennon

Saying Goodbye to an Old Friend

The Santa Barbara haven lasted ten days. By then a combination of three fires were sending smoke over the surrounding mountains and pouring into the city.

It was not an uneventful period though. It saw the passing of my eminently reliable Corolla Station Wagon. The car died a loud death at a quiet Santa Barbara intersection. I had brought the vehicle to rest at a 4-way stop and upon letting out the clutch, a few seconds worth of sounds of metal parts grinding away at each other emitted from the transmission. And that was that. The wheels on my beloved car no longer went round and round.

It was expected the car would have been in the family forever. Older corolla wagons are in demand due to excellent reliability, bargain pricing, good cargo capacity and decent fuel economy. There are fewer and fewer of these gems on the road and I had no plans to ever let this one go. As it happened I had a Tesla Model 3 on order –the lower cost, down-sized version of the popular pure electric Model S- and once the Model 3 appeared in the driveway sometime in 2018 or so, the Corolla would have been the designated backup vehicle. Living so far from civilization makes having a backup car a good idea.

Alas, being hundreds of miles from home, receiving repair quotes that exceeded the value of the car, and having no good place to store the vehicle until it could be towed home to drydock brought forth a heart wrenching decision; Sell the car as-is and buy a new one.

I phoned three dealerships; Toyota, Honda, and Nissan. The Honda folks were all in a meeting, so, you-snooze-you-lose. Nissan had some attractive year-end deals on various models, but the winner on pricing was Toyota with a fantastic year-end clearance sale on a Prius.

A Prius. Hmm. The way-popular hybrid vehicle that I had never stepped foot in. Since I never buy new cars any more a Prius had never been on the radar. My purchases are normally confined to 20-year old Hondas or Toyotas, and no Prius is that old. But when you need a car now you need it **now**. No time to shop the Auto Trader, and I'm reticent to buy used cars from auto dealers (they don't know the car's history).

The nice people at Santa Barbara Toyota sent a salesman to the house to bring me to the dealership. The key word in that last sentence is "nice". They actually are decent folks there. In fact, I would label the two to three hours spent test driving, deciding, completing the paperwork, and receiving the keys to my BRAND NEW CAR as the least painful experience at an automobile dealership ever.

Note: I had initially test driven a smaller version of the standard sized Prius designated the 'Prius C', which I immediately renamed the mini-me. I also test drove a couple of traditional gas powered models, which were tempting, but at the last minute veered to the full-sized Prius. Completely unbeknownst to me at the time of purchase was that in two short weeks I would be employing that Prius in the service of Uber Technologies, and the choice to buy a 5-passenger, super-high gas mileage car with decent cargo space would turn out to be a great case of "blind luck".

Exodus Number Two

Life with a BRAND NEW CAR was wonderful, but now there was a new fire on the radar. On August 13th word came that the "Chimney" fire had broken out some 40 miles southeast of Big Sur. The smoke was trending southward, blending with the smoke from the Soberanes fire already drifting toward Santa Barbara. By August 19th the smoke from both fires crossed the mountains bordering the north end of Santa Barbara. My lungs were crying uncle as the blue haze visible in the foothills had its effect. Furthermore the "Rey" fire just to the east of Santa Barbara had broken out that same day. It was time to evacuate again.

I packed up the car and proceeded to ... where? Where was there to go? North? No way. East? Not a chance. South? I suppose so, but I really didn't want to get too far from home. Pondering... pondering... wait. Aha. Lompoc!

FIVE
HOW I LEARNED TO STOP WORRYING AND LOVE UBER

Lompoc
Man Converts to Uberism
Uber James' First Night
The Goodie Strategy
Uber James' First Day
Uber Stories:
Uber James Gets Summoned to Freedom... Then to Purgatory
Halfway Home
Air Mobile to the Rescue
Birds of a Feather
Exodus Number Three

"When you come to a fork in the road, take it"
- Yogi Berra

Arriving in Lompoc

Lompoc is a smallish coastal city off the beaten path about an hour north and west of Santa Barbara (see map on pg. 9). I knew of the town from doing overnight stays there years ago when traveling from San Francisco to Los Angeles on business. Lompoc resides on the lesser traveled coast route Highway 1 (most traffic at that latitude traverses Hwy 101). The city came to mind because it is way off to the west, residing on an outcropping of land that just might have been clear of the prevailing winds pushing the smoke down from the north.

The theory turned out to be correct. Lompoc sort of has its own isolated weather system. From the downtown area I could see a veil of smoke enshrouding the so-called Lompoc Hills to the east, but that was about as close as the smoky air was encroaching on the city limits.

Lompoc has always been known for agriculture and flowers, which are grown in the moderately sized Lompoc Valley. But in the quarter of a century since I had last passed through the town things had changed, and I was soon to learn that there was depth to this micro-metropolis not immediately apparent.

I made a deal with a budget motel within the city limits for a weekly rate and bivouacked there for what would turn out to be about a month. Watching budget motel TV -with its limited channel selections- after having sworn off the boob-tube for fifteen years was maddening. I wasn't sure what was more irritating, the commercials or the programs. An alternative to television had to be found. There was no possibility of hanging out with friends to escape the TV, given that I had no friends in Lompoc. Hanging out at bars had zero appeal.

Since last visiting, the Lompoc city forefathers had approved a series of giant murals to be painted on the sides of buildings around town. It was enjoyable to seek them all out. Remarkable artistry.

One of many building murals in downtown Lompoc

Another idea was to investigate every restaurant in town in order to determine where the finest local cuisine was to be had. The tactic was to simply go and eat at all of them. This was fun. Within two weeks I had locked onto the best Thai restaurant (Herb Home Thai), and gotten a handle on the best hole-in-the-wall Mexican food (El Palmar). There were a few sushi places in town but I'm leery about applying the same sort of shotgun methodology to sushi. A few folks gave recommendations but I ended up passing. Pinning down the best burger joint was next on the agenda, but that line of inquiry was never fully investigated.

Man Converts to Uberism

The restaurant recon was fun but you can't eat *all* the time. Finally a solution hit me. Uber. From my ensconced, unplugged perch in Big Sur, which is mostly free of cell towers, I had heard rumors of a service enabling citizens to give other citizens a ride in their personal car. The technology of hand-held internet devices had made this possible. People could summon a ride with a mere few presses of the touch screen on their smartphone. Fascinating.

There are quite a few ride-sharing companies but a quick google scan revealed that only Uber was operating in Lompoc. "That's it!", I said to myself. "I'm going to sign up for Uber. Right this minute."

Why the excitement? Why did this decision get made immediately and without a pondering delay?

*"Because I was harboring a life-long desire
to drive a taxicab."*

I always thought driving a taxi would be a cool job. Independence. Simplicity. Driving people from point A to point B. Also, I love to drive. I am more content behind the wheel than almost any other endeavor. Driving, albeit cars, motor homes, or preferably motorcycles, is my Zen. When driving I'm relaxed and at peace with the world.

Plus, during my IT career I would dream about having a simpler kind of job. Owning your own business is kind of a full time job in and of itself. You not only have to be a master of your art, you have to constantly be drumming up business. There's the paperwork. The taxes. The workers. Plus, providing IT services in particular means constantly going back to school in order to keep up with the stream of new technologies. So at times I fantasized about giving it all up. The thought of driving people from point A to point B in a taxi had quite the allure.

I also dreamed about owning a Christmas tree farm. A cut-your-own farm.

But the IT career held fast. It was great work, really. I was blessed with a handful of Fortune 500 clients and a six figure income. It was a good gig so the taxi driver job remained a fantasy.

But now, mostly retired from that line of work, being on the road, and with the Uber service making it so darned easy to be a cabbie.... this was a no-brainer decision. Uber was the missing link that would provide a means to occupy my mind and allow me to stop worrying about hemorrhaging cash.

By the end of the day I was officially driving for Uber Technologies Inc. I uploaded a copy of my driver's license, vehicle registration, and proof of insurance. The Uber folks ran my DMV record and performed some sort of background check. That was it. I was good to go by nightfall.

This is not to say that Uber is at all lackadaisical about qualifying drivers. It's just that I was likely a good candidate. The company requires an Uber car to be less than eight years old. Not a problem, given that I owned a BRAND NEW CAR. I had a clean DMV, a spot-free criminal background, and no overdue books at the library. In fact, I've been known to help my landlady carry out her garbage. But in my view the best qualification one can have to drive Uber is years and years of experiencing poor customer service. This gives one perspective on the importance of proper customer service.

Uber James' First Night

So here it is the evening of the day I sign up. An email comes in from Uber saying I'm good to go. The Uber driver app has already been downloaded. I slide the slider from **OFFLINE** to **ONLINE**. And guess what happened?

Someone wanted a ride! I swear, within a second or two of going online the driver app lit up. A black screen with a white circle appeared. The screen was flashing repeatedly and making a sound reminiscent of a sonar ping.

"Wait. What? This thing actually works?!"

Apparently, yes. Someone wanted a ride, and they were expecting **me**, the soon to be self-named *Uber James*, to come and pick them up. Amazing.

There was only one problem. I wasn't ready. Mainly, the car was full of my personal stuff. This was Friday night and I was in the habit of checking out of my motel on the weekends to save money. The only free space in the Prius was the front passenger seat.

I set the car in motion and prayed for a solo rider. I didn't recognize the pickup address and had no city map, but there was a button on the driver app labeled **Navigate**. I pushed the button and Google Maps launched. A female voice started barking orders. I did exactly what she said, and seven minutes and a few turns later the Prius was parked in front of the address. Two young adults were standing in the street, a man and a woman.

Yikes. Two people. I had to think fast. One of them had already opened the back door and the expressions on each of their faces were starting to reflect the fact that there was nowhere to sit.

Uber James: "Oh. Uh. Just a sec. Uh. Ok. Here's the deal. I just signed up for Uber and then I got this ride request rather instantly. I'm so sorry but I'm not really set up yet. Tell you what. We can cancel this ride and you can call for another car.... or... if someone wants to sit on the other's lap I will take you to your destination at no charge."

Girl rider: "OK. We'll sit in front."

While uttering excuses I had noticed the two people were likely a couple. It turned out they were, and that's why the ploy probably worked. Phew.

We drove the 10 minutes to the rider's destination. The kids got out. I think they were getting ready to say goodbye without bothering to inquire about a refund. At this point in time I did not know how easy it is to refund the rider so I pulled a twenty out of my wallet and offered it to the pair.

Uber James: "I'm sorry, I don't know how to keep you from being charged. The ride cannot possibly be more than $20. This being my first fare I really want to get a 5-star rating, so I hope you are happy."

Girl rider: "OK. Thanx. We'll definitely give you 5 stars."

They took the bill. A 5-star rating did appear on the app later. I also later learned that the fare was just over $6 for that ride. And the pair probably had known that.

Live and learn. But what was it about my apparent need for a 5-star rating in that situation? This is an interesting topic. My initial impetus to get all 5-star ratings was, uh, ego I suppose. It just seemed like a fun game to play. Give riders such great service that they in-turn give you the highest possible rating. Without ever having consciously thought of it I knew my short career as an Uber driver was going to be about hopefully giving riders an exemplary experience whisking them from point A to point B.

This latent impulse stemmed from two organic sources. For one thing, I had been a very poor student back in school. C average is putting it politely. After flunking high school algebra twice my teacher gave me a courtesy D just to get me out of the class. I actually had to take an extra semester of auto shop to graduate high school. Later, in my twenties, a friend and I took a beginning class in a computer programming language, and I got an A in the course. Something clicked in my brain during that class and I've since gotten nothing but As in all subsequent schooling of any kind. Anything less is quite unacceptable. So it was sort of built-in that all 5-star ratings was the only option driving for Uber.

Secondly, as mentioned, I'm the very first one to complain about how bad customer service has gotten in America. Having someone who cares enough to go to the trouble of actually solving your problem is a rarity. Usually it's all about the fluff of *acting* like great customer service is being rendered ("Is there anything else I can do for you today?"), when in fact the problem you called about often lingers until a second, or maybe third call is initiated. So now that that *I* was the one providing the customer service I'd darned well better do an A+ job. *Because I understand how much it means to people.*

So I say to myself, "Here is your chance to put your money where your mouth is. I will try and give each and every rider a superb experience transporting them from point A to point B. I'm going to arrive promptly for pickups. I'm going to smile at everyone... even people who creep me out. I'm going to hold the door for all fares. I'm going to drive in an exemplary fashion that gives all passengers the feeling of being shuttled to their destination swiftly, yet safely."

The Goodie Strategy

After dropping off that first fare I went **OFFLINE** and headed to the 99-cent store. Lompoc has a 99-cent store and a Dollar Tree Store. I found myself wondering why anyone would shop at a Dollar store when there is a 99-cent store two blocks away. Anyway, it's off to the 99-cent store to buy a 99-cent Tupperware type container. The vessel is then filled full of 99-cent candy... Werther's original Caramel Coffee Hard Candies, Ocean Spray Craisins, a variety of gum, and even some Halls cough drops in case someone has a sore throat. A couple of 6 packs of bottled water are procured for... you guessed it... 99-cent each.

The candy/gum box goes in the middle of the back seat. The water bottles go in the handy dandy water bottle holders built into each door. Thank you Toyota. Also acquired were charging cords for both iPhones and Android devices. When a fare gets into the car I point out that the goodies are for them, at no charge. I sit back and observe how people respond to this offer. Reactions run the gamut. Some folks say thank you, but never touch the goodies. At the other end of the spectrum people literally assault the candy/gum box. The favorite item is the Werther's. Starburst "the unexplainably juicy candy" is added later and the Starburst's knock the Werther's out of first place. Gum always runs a close second.

Some people, upon being notified of the goodies exclaim; "Ok. 5 stars." With the goodie strategy in place it was really mine to lose. Meaning, just get the passenger safely from point A to point B with minimal delay, don't say/do anything stupid, and everythin's gonna be all right.

Uber James' First Day

The next morning there were a few things to get in order, Uber-wise. I needed to find a place to store all the stuff in the back seat and hatchback area. For now I was sleeping in my car on weekends because the motel rates exploded on Friday and Saturday nights.

When I had first hit town the owner of a local mailing facility had befriended me. His name was Bob and his handle was 'Box Shop Bob', because his store was called 'The Box Shop'. Not to be confused with 'Sideshow Bob' of The Simpsons, Box Shop Bob was running one of the highest volume UPS stores in the state. I was having my mail forwarded to The Box Shop so was down there often, and Bob and I had struck up a rapport. Bob had sympathetically listened to my tale about being self-evacuated from two communities because of the fires, and how I had chosen Lompoc because it was out of the smoke corridor.

So now it was off to The Box Shop, car full of luggage and miscellany, to inquire as to whether Bob could store the gear. For a fee. He said sure. No fee. Bob was excited about the whole driving-for-Uber idea to earn me some money while in town and was happy to support the endeavor.

While at the store I was able to print some temporary Uber

"trade dress" which is a fancy term for the Uber signs you have to place at the front and back of the car. To skip that step invited rider confusion and a $1,000 fine if the cops nailed you driving Uber without them. Uber promised to mail me the permanent laminated signs, informing me that the paper temps would hold me over till they arrived.

What else? Passengers have the driver's first name before they enter the car, but it hit me that some kind of nickname might make the driver seem more approachable. The best I could come up with was 'Uber James'. It was kind of a lame handle but it turned out people liked it. They would laugh and play it back. "Uber James. Ha ha." If someone called me just James that was fine, but in the right circumstances I would retort in a mock serious voice "That's *Uber James* to you." That always got a laugh too.

Lompoc Uber Stories

I'll tell you right now that if I had only driven Uber in Lompoc there would be no book. Driving there was a rather placid experience. Daytime fares were dominated by folks going to and from work. For a variety of reasons some people don't have a car to get to work. It might be for economic reasons, car in shop, DUI, etc. In this respect Uber has been a godsend. Imagine not having to bug a friend every day, or hitchhike, or take a more expensive taxi. As a matter of fact when you add up all the costs to own and maintain an automobile, Uber may be a money saver.

Nighttime fares were mostly bar pickups. At the end of the first week I knew where every watering hole in town was. Those fares went pretty well considering the clientele was intoxicated. But that's the idea, right? There was never any trouble. I did pick up a drunk once who had the hiccups. He hiccupped non-stop the entire 20 minute ride home.

Uber Story   🚗   Uber Story   🚗   Uber Story

Uber James Gets Summoned to Freedom...
Then to Purgatory

One day the Uber driver app lit up with a request for an out of town pickup. The address was south of Lompoc off the road that goes to Jalama Beach, a famous remote surfing and camping spot to the southwest. Driving down Jalama Road the navigator had me turn onto a dirt road leading toward some foothills. I had absolutely no idea where I was going or when I would get there. The Uber driver app estimates the minutes to reach the pickup spot but I hadn't gotten in the habit of looking, partially because all fares up till then were no more than 10 minutes away, and partially because I was trying to maneuver my BRAND NEW CAR down a narrow, winding dirt road.

Note: Keep in mind that I normally live in area so remote there is no cell service. No cell service means no smart phones. No smart phones means no google maps and navigation. This whole world of Uber, maps, Waze, and turn-by-turn navigation was a new realm. I had made a successful career as an IT consultant, yet was completely naïve to this brand of tech.

Before long a few wooden structures appeared. It was a ranch. As I eased forward to drive past the first building I spotted a lone woman sitting on a bench placed tight up against a dilapidated barn. There were no other humans in site. The young woman was dressed to the height of western fashion; dark blue jeans covering a pair of long legs, a red and white checkered shirt, a bandana, and of course a cowboy hat partially covering a mane of blonde hair. She was Scandinavian looking. And with the weathered wood of the red barn acting as a canvas it was really quite a picture. A magazine cover, really.

She smiled as I crawled by but didn't utter a word. "Is that my fare?" I wonder. I continue creeping forward a few yards and at the end of the barn came to a stop. Inadvertently the word "wow" came out of my mouth. I looked in the rearview mirror and could see the girl looking my way, smiling a larger smile.

Looking left past the barn some horses and some other humans were now visible about twenty feet away. It was two women and a man. I looked at them. They looked at me. One of the women waved and cried out "Uber?" I responded in the affirmative. They did not move toward the car though. Still some conversation to wrap up.

What should I do? Go over there? That would be intruding. Wait by the car? Yes. Wait unless summoned. I popped out of the car and opened the back doors. It was unclear how many of this group were going on the ride. All four would fit, and that was the main thing. Then the man picked up a cluster of bags. Unwieldy bags. Not standard issue luggage. The group of three moved toward the car. It turned out just the man needed a ride. He filled the hatchback full of his gear, issued a few hugs to the women, said a few more goodbyes, then hopped in the front seat and we were off.

Note: It became a point of interest when picking up singles whether they would get in the front or the back. Most people, surprisingly, sit in the front. Men and women both. Another departure from the taxicab culture?

As we pulled out I reached for the phone and started the ride.

It was then that I saw we were going to the Santa Barbara Airport. Santa Barbara has the closest large airport to Lompoc. It is a solid 45 minute ride so this was going to be a profitable fare.

But at the same time my lungs were freaking out at the prospect of the destination. A few weeks ago I had escaped that smoke purgatory. What would the air quality be like now? The ride *could* be cancelled, but I had adopted a policy early on of accepting every ride request and taking the fare wherever they wished to go.

So off we went to the airport. I had an N95 mask stashed in the center console for just such occasions. The fare turned out to be a very friendly gentleman with an interesting story. He was a photographer. The ranch was a wild horse sanctuary called 'Return to Freedom' (**returntofreedom.org**), and the photographer had flown in from the east coast to shoot all week at the ranch. Something to do with publicizing the noble work being done there.

Horses of Return to Freedom Ranch

The time to the airport passed quickly as my chatty passenger went on about how excited he was to have photographed the sanctuary. I of course had to ask him about the beautiful woman sitting against the barn. He had met her. She was indeed from some Scandinavian country. Something had happened to the girl. Something traumatic. I forget how big or how little, but quite honestly it wouldn't be fair to the young lady to repeat regardless. She was there at the ranch as a volunteer out of a love of horses. I got the impression that the ranch was a healing place for her.

The Santa Barbara run went well. It was shaping up that short bursts of smoke while wearing the mask was doable.

Uber Story   🚗   Uber Story   🚗   Uber Story

Halfway Home

Another somewhat common destination for riders heading out of town was the train station. There is a teeny tiny AMTRAK station fifteen minutes west of Lompoc. The tracks parallel the Pacific Ocean. From the station, called 'Surf', you can take the Pacific Surfliner north to San Luis Obispo or south to Santa Barbara and beyond.

It was in picking up a fare bound for the station that I learned Lompoc had a Halfway House. The Prius was summoned to a non-descript building a few blocks from the city administration center. It was a commercial looking building with no signage. A younger man was saying his farewells to an older man. The younger man then headed to the car and took a seat in the front after stowing a small amount of luggage in the back seat. The destination came up as the Amtrak Surf Station and off we went.

What do you say to a young person who has just gotten released from a halfway house? Well first, I knew what the building was because he told me. He was kind of poking around at having a conversation. I kind of laid back, saying just enough to encourage him to continue. He relaxed and shared enough information to where I could see he was dealing with the fact he was on his own now and whatever work he had done at the house was now going to be tested. It was back to the real world.

It was also clear that the man, in his early-twenties, was grappling with the idea of how he was going to stay out of trouble... contemplating how he would avoid the temptation of returning to his old ways. He never said exactly what he had gotten into trouble for and I didn't ask. At some level it simply didn't matter, and certainly not at the level we two were conversing on a taxi ride to a train station.

I tried to avoid blurting out the standard issue advice about how to stay out of trouble (discipline, avoid bad company, etc.). Twenty years ago I would have said that. But having learned over time that life has a way of throwing whatever it's going to throw at you regardless -whether it be fate, destiny, or karma- I'm a little more circumspect these days about giving such advice. There may be, for lack of better words, a deeper wisdom to pass on in these circumstances.

So I told him the one thing I tell myself these days when trouble comes. It's one of maybe two or three wisdom nuggets that have stuck with me. I told him:

"Whatever comes... use it"

Whatever is sent your way, even if it's really bad, try to find a way to make use of the *opportunity*. Turn it around. Leverage it in your favor. For example, if someone is a total ass to you, don't react, make that person your teacher. They are not teaching you how to be... they are demonstrating through their actions how *not* to be. That's powerful. Don't fight back. Don't personalize the conflict. Take the lesson and thank them, if only in your head.

I've learned over the years that this advice -which is really just another way of saying make lemonade from lemons- may be one of the few pieces of general advice that can work for anyone. Because we are each on our own path, much "tried and true" advice might work fine for one person but backfire for another.

"Whatever comes... use it." The young man smiled a bit as the words bounced around his brain and then out his mouth. "OK", he said. Then we were at the station. We made firm eye contact –a bit of a rarity when driving Uber- shook hands, and off he went to the next chapter.

Uber Story   🚗   Uber Story   🚗   Uber Story

Air Mobile to the Rescue

One of the most interesting fares I got in Lompoc was a military pickup. The request came in from one of the better motels on the north end of town. When I pulled into the entranceway the fare was ready and waiting near the door of the lobby. This was unusual for a motel pickup. Quite often there is a delay as the passengers are still in their room preparing for the outing. But these guys were fully prepped. Three males. Military. Army, to be precise. One man was in fatigues. That was the giveaway. He sat in front. Pure military through and through. He sort of looked like R. Lee Ermey, the Marine Corp Staff Sergeant turned actor who's played parts as a military man in movies such as Full Metal Jacket (as Gunnery Sergeant Hartman), and as the voice of Sarge in Toy Story 3.

The other two men were dressed in civilian clothes but their haircuts gave *them* away. Lompoc is a military town as well as an agriculture center. Just north of the city is Vandenberg Air Force base, the west coast launch facility for the now retired Space Shuttle. The base is still bustling however. Missiles are launched there on a regular basis and Vandenberg is home to

SpaceX, the upstart cutting edge rocket design and manufac-
turing company founded by Elon Musk of Tesla fame. In town
it is not uncommon to see military types supporting local businesses. In fact there are a number of tattoo parlors and window
tinting establishments that exist solely due to the presence of
the military.

I'd been picking up military fares on a regular basis during my
Uber tour of Lompoc. Often, but not always from bars. I liked
such pickups. The military lads and lasses were always well
behaved, even if they had spent the evening trying to fill a
hollow leg with beer. But again, that's what Uber's there for. It
turned out the base had a zero-tolerance, take-no-prisoners
policy against drinking and driving. Word had it that any
personnel showing up at the gate intoxicated was asking for
trouble. So quite often I would transport the jolly crews
through the gate and right to their quarters on base.

But as mentioned, the gentlemen who had just fastened themselves in the Prius weren't Air Force. They were Army.
"What's up with that", I ask, breaking the ice. The uniformed
man in the front seat sporting sergeant stripes responded. It
turned out these guys were here to help put out the fires! Recall
that at least three major fires are burning out of control in the
central part of the state; two to the northeast and one to the
southeast. Governor Jerry Brown had declared California a
disaster area, and by doing so had opened the door to Federal
funding to put the fires out. And guess what came along with
that funding? Military support. These boys were part of a crew
that fueled the helicopters fighting the fires. That was their
entire job: putting jet fuel in helicopters. The crew was based
out of Sacramento, and when word came down to assist in the
firefighting efforts the base had flown in a passel of Blackhawks
to bivouac at the Santa Ynez airport. The airport, twenty five

miles east of Lompoc, had been partially taken over as a base for fire related air operations.

Blackhawks, eh? My civilian mind was immediately filled with images of Mogadishu and the movie Blackhawk Down. So, I had to ask the question. I knew the answer but I just *had* to ask... for the record...

Uber James: "So I assume the helicopters fighting the fire have no weapons, correct?"

The sergeant: "Correct. As a matter of fact they never have weapons attached at all when in country. It is only when they are shipped overseas and have been brought onto the field of battle that the choppers are fitted with weapons."

It was nice to learn that the military's kinda careful about weapons and stuff. On the other hand, having one of those standard issue 6,000 rounds per minute, 7.62 mm, six-barreled M134 Mini-guns on board might have come in handy if the chopper happened across the idiots who started the fire. But, that's just me.

By the way, upon starting out on the trip I had learned the crew was destined for a bar in Santa Ynez called the Maverick Saloon. Santa Ynez was to the east and well inside the smoke belt. During the entire time I'd been conversing with the sergeant, panic was also lapping at the shores of my brain because anything east of Lompoc was off limits for my lungs. Unfortunately there is no way to tell the Uber driver app of destinations you do **not** want to drive fares to. You can't map out the geographic area you wish to Uber in. But, I had my trusty mask, short trips to Santa Barbara had worked out, so inside my head the encouraging phrase "Damn the smoke. Full speed ahead" was playing to counter the fright.

At some point I learned why the sergeant was in uniform. Free beers. Simple as that. The saloon would supply anyone in uniform with free beers. It was a very patriotic establishment! Plus the entire Santa Ynez Valley knew it was flirting with disaster. The only thing that laid between the valley and the encroaching fires were a few mountains, a handful of miles, and the hard working fire crews. As an example of community support for the firefighters, the owner of a local Holiday Inn Express was giving free lodging to the crews. Free lodging, *at the height of the summer tourist season.* The street in front of the hotel was lined with fire trucks every night.

I never saw those Army guys again that evening. Taken home by another Uber car no doubt.

Uber Story   🚗   Uber Story   🚗   Uber Story

Birds of a Feather

One day I got a fare that turned out to be another Uber driver. He was changing the brakes on his own Uber car and needed a ride to the machine shop to *turn the rotors.* It's a task that's part of a complete brake job. We got to talking and I learned that Lompoc didn't have enough action for him. He drove down to Santa Barbara each day to catch fares. The gentleman was supporting a family with his Uber income.

The guy had it that the average life expectancy of an Uber driver is three months. The statistic was made believable upon learning that the Achilles Heel of trying to make a go of it driving for Uber is **Mileage**. He and other drivers I've run into always have some sort of story about how they are dealing with the incredible amount of miles that pile up on their personal vehicles. The stories usually have to do with getting a second car or working out a way to buy a new car and have it still be under warranty when the last payment is made. More on this later.

The driver showed me his car on the way back from the machine shop. He had rigged up a camera system below the rearview mirror that took continuous footage looking forward as well as backward. In other words he was filming his passengers. He wasn't a weirdo or anything. This was for safety. Uber drivers sometimes have trouble get in the car along with the passengers. This driver was making sure that if trouble happened there would be a recording.

For a while I thought about installing a similar rig, but in the end chose not to. I wasn't worried about that kind of trouble. My biggest fear was that someone would barf in my BRAND NEW CAR and it didn't matter much if such an event was videotaped. Other kinds of trouble... meh. I felt I could handle whatever came up. It's not like I have a Lightsaber hidden under my robes or anything. It's just that I've learned over the years what kind of trouble comes my way and what kind doesn't. It's almost like everyone is magnetized in some way. There are certain things you attract and certain things you don't. It varies for each of us. I just happen to not attract *that* kind of trouble. This may be an arrogant or naïve point of view, but as it happens in the one thousand trips that summer and fall, the worst thing that occurred *in* the car was a small handful of near-barf experiences. I was very lucky and I count my blessings, on all fronts. For the worse thing that happened *outside* the car see Chapter 13.

Oh. That other Uber driver told me one funny thing I'll never forget. He had a way to make his driver app sound off whenever his wife wanted him to do some work around the house. He would trigger his phone to make it sound like he was getting a fare request. Oops. Gotta go. (Dude, if you buy this book be sure to tear out this page before leaving it laying around the house)

Exodus Number Three

Things continued to go well in Lompoc. After a month or so the whole Uber thing and the supporting technology was feeling second nature. I had learned the lay of the land and was picking up fares faster than you can say blueberry pancakes. The only thing at all unnerving was that every once in a while the drivers app would light up with a ride request for Santa Ynez or its neighboring cities Solvang and Buellton. These cities were all in Smokeville. I stubbornly refused to ignore the ride request though, and would drive the twenty to thirty minutes to retrieve the passenger. Although the temporary exposure to smoke did leave me a bit queasy now and then, smoke in the valley was abating over time.

Then one day I opened the door of my Lompoc motel room to find the sky full of smoke. The fourth fire affecting my life had lit off. It was on the Air Force base and had been sparked by some broken power lines hitting the dry grass.

The fire was close. Only a few miles away. There was only one possible course of action. I packed up all my stuff, got in the car, and drove east.

SIX

UBER STORIES FROM WINE COUNTRY

I'm not Taking People to Work... I'm Taking Them to Play
Uber Stories:
The Stranded Boyfriend
The Stranded Girlfriend
The Stranded Wine Tasters
Uber James' First Wine Fare
The Three Happy Nurses
Next Stop... The Twilight Zone

"Are you not entertained?"
- Maximus Decimus Meridius

I'm not Taking People to Work... I'm Taking Them to Play

Me and the Prius are galloping toward the Santa Ynez Valley. Over the weeks the smoke was abating from the valley as the fires were surrounded by containment lines. I had fared well the last few trips over from Lompoc and there were few other hideouts left save evacuating the central coast entirely. Could my discombobulated lungs fare well in the Santa Ynez Valley?

Yes. It worked out. There were still *mask days* on occasion but the air progressively improved. On smoky days I'd always show up for a fare mask-less, and then put it on once underway. Passengers were very understanding, often quoting their own respiratory issues. The mask was never an issue, but I always let the fare see my face first.

I found a good cheap motel in the quaint town of Solvang and made a weekly deal with the property owner. My whole *uber world* was now about the Santa Ynez Valley. It wasn't too long after relocating operations to the valley that a realization hit me:

"I'm not taking people to work. I'm taking them to play"

The valley was a whole different paradigm. People were almost always smiling when they got in the car. They were in the valley by choice and were relaxed, some from the idea of being on vacation, and some due to a little help from the spirits. Not that there's anything wrong with that! Of course a certain percent of rides were locals shuttling to/from work, running errands, going out to dinner safely, etc. I liked having locals in the car. They too were usually in a good mood, and always had plenty of stories to help round out my knowledge of the area.

I was also becoming aware of an emerging theme that would dominate the remainder of my time driving in the valley. It was happening in Lompoc a bit, but now was becoming quite evident; *People want to know about their driver*! Almost universally, when a fare got in the car they would inquire about where I was from, how I happen to be driving for Uber, etc. This is the antithesis of the taxicab mindset. I can't tell you how many times I've recited my *man evacuated from home, chased around the state, turns to Uber to pay travel expenses* saga. And it's not because I was dying to tell people the story. Rather it went something like this:

Passenger: *"Are you from here?"*

Uber James: *"No. I just drive for Uber here."*

Passenger: *"Oh. Where are you from?"*

Uber James: *"Big Sur."*

Passenger: *"Oh I/we LOVE Big Sur. Isn't it a long drive to come here to Uber?"*

Uber James: *"Well I don't commute. I'm staying here in the valley for a while."*

Passenger: *"Oh. How come you're away from home?"*

Uber James: *"Well, there is a big forest fire there right now and I am evacuated."*

From there the passengers would expresses sympathy (thank you all, it helped), and I then either imparted the entire odyssey, or we talked about the fire, or the passenger would tell me about their visit to Big Sur that year or the year before. It was astonishing how many passengers had not only visited Big Sur, but had done so in recent memory.

Shying away from divulging the evacuation story didn't really work, as people would keep inquiring until they got me to fess up. If for example I implied that I was staying in the valley that would not suffice. They would *always* pick up on "staying here" as opposed to "I live here" and dig further. Unless I were to outright lie, which I chose not to do, the story would always be coaxed out.

But at the core of that curiosity is a passenger's desire to gain some familiarity with their driver. I actually had fares tell me they had become uncomfortable on other Uber rides when the driver declined to engage them in conversation. I guess you could explain this behavior any number of ways. The whole thing with Uber is that your "neighbor" is giving you a lift. They're not a professional driver. It's the guy you've seen at Wal-Mart. It's the gal that works at the post office by day. In other words, it's someone like you. And, ride sharing is still relatively new. It's still this bright shiny object that fascinates us. How can it be so affordable? How can it work so well? How did we ever get by without smart phones!?

Yes, how did we?

Uber Story   🚗   Uber Story   🚗   Uber Story

The Stranded Boyfriend

One of the earliest and more memorable valley fares occurred the first week of driving in Solvang. It was late in the evening. I was tiring, and thinking of going offline. Suddenly the phone lit up with a ride request. As usual I poked at the screen to accept it, not even noticing the pickup location. I stuffed my key fob in its standard location: left pants pocket, pulled on my vest, stuffed my phone in its left hand pocket, my wallet in the right, and walked the thirty feet to the car. Everything else required for a ride was already in the Prius.

Upon checking the app for the pickup address a surprise was waiting. All the app said was "Highway 101." No actual address. Just Hwy 101. OK. The freeway was about four miles west in Buellton. The GPS should guide me to the person's exact location. And if need be I would call.

The thing is, I was learning not to trust GPS too much. It's great for helping navigate to the general area of the pickup, but not always for fine work. I've had the Uber driver app take me within 50 feet of the fare's house... but on the other side of a creek. So there was no substitute for a solid physical address. In this case the plan was to call the fare once I got near the freeway to determine their exact location. The fare had the same idea however and phoned me first.

Uber James: "Hello?"

Fare: "Is this Uber? I'm on the freeway."

Uber James: "What?"

Fare: "I'm on the freeway. But I'm not near any freeway exit."

Uber James: "Well what was the last freeway exit you passed?"

Fare: <pause> ... "I don't know. It's really dark here. Are you going to be able to find me?"

Uber James: "I'll find you. I will call you when I get close."

Fare: "The battery on my phone is dying. It's at 3%."

Uber James: "OK. Once the GPS says I'm close I will flash my lights. You do the same."

Fare: "OK."

We hang up. Per the GPS signal I steered the trusty Uber car onto the northbound onramp of the freeway. The navigation app WAZE is trying to help (on a tip from a passenger I had switched from Google Maps to WAZE). All this time I'm thinking the guy must have had his car conk out on him. All I have to do is spot a car on the shoulder. Unsure which side of the freeway the guy was on, I drive in the fast lane in order to have the best view of the shoulders on either side of the highway. It's near midnight, the freeway is a mortuary, and it's really really dark. I keep driving. WAZE tells me I'm close. No vehicle to be found though.

Suddenly there is a barely visible light up ahead. It's coming from the center divider. I slow and flash my lights. As the car rolls by what's revealed is a man pressed up against the divider from the other side of the freeway. His light source is a cigarette lighter. I yell to the guy to wait over on the shoulder while I go up and find a turnaround. The car lurches forward. The rearview mirror indicates the man is complying. I find an open spot to cross over and whip the car around to the south-bound lanes. Easing forward I spot the man on the shoulder, again with the lighter waving around. But there's something missing.

Uber James: "Where's your car??"

Fare: "There is no car."

Uh huh. The man gets in, the Prius gets up to speed, and we talk for a minute while he warms up. He plugs his phone in to charge. I should mention that when I talked to him on the phone his voiced sounded stressed. Now in the car I was looking at a guy who was pretty shaken up. He wasn't freaking out or anything, but there was enough of a vibe to shift me into speak-in-a-calm-reassuring-voice mode. The man's story now came out. He had been in a car with a woman he was dating and things had turned sour. They had left his car behind in L.A. and taken her car up to Pismo Beach (about an hour north of Buellton) in order to retrieve some items from her friend's house. On the way back from Pismo a fight had broken out and the guy claimed to have "jumped out of the car."

The man showed no outward signs of having jumped from a vehicle at freeway speeds, so presumably his gal had slowed down enough to let him leap from the car without incurring serious injuries. But if his body wasn't bruised his ego was. He needed to tell me the entire story of what had transpired. He *needed* to. As we close in on Buellton there's just one thing on *my* mind: Where did he want me to take him (presumably to the nearest motel)? But he wasn't ready to focus on that yet. He kept telling me the story of what had unfolded between himself and this girl. So, I listened. There is no high drama here about what unfolded. As best I recall, except for the jumping out of the car part it was a sort of standard issue boyfriend/girlfriend type blowout. There was a disagreement. Someone felt they were being treated unfairly. Tempers flared. Man exits car prematurely.

Once the gentleman had finished the story he breathed a sigh of relief. The man lightened up considerably and was now able to get down to the business at hand.

Fare: "Thanks for listening! I just needed to get that off my chest."

Uber James: "No problem."

Fare: "This whole event has been unnerving. I only had enough of a charge to make one phone call. I decided to call for an Uber. It felt good to hear a calm voice when I called. That helped a lot."

Uber James: "No problem................ Do you have an idea where you want to go? We're almost to Buellton and we can find you a motel for the night. If you want I can take you back to L.A. in the morning."

Fare: "No. I need to get back tonight. I have to give a presentation at work in the morning. Can you take me?"

(This was a tough one dear readers. Uber James hates to say no!)

Uber James: "No. I can't do that. Only because I'm too tired. Would it help if I took you to Santa Barbara?"

Fare: "Yes! Definitely. Let's go."

Santa Barbara was 45 minutes south. I felt up to the round trip. If I fell apart at SB I could always lay over and return to Solvang in the AM. In the front passenger seat my fare jumped on his freshly charged phone and made arrangements for a friend to start driving up from L.A. and meet him in SB. We made it to town without incident. The handoff took place at a 24hr Denny's. And that was that.

Uber Story 🚗 Uber Story 🚗 Uber Story

The Stranded Girlfriend

Here is a quick story that actually ties into the prior one. This was a fare much later in the season. It was a woman who did some part time Uber driving herself in Santa Barbara. Having no knowledge of my stranded-on-the-freeway story she told me of a similar incident with one of her fare's.... except in this case it was a *female* stranded on the freeway. Yikes.

The lady Uber driver also had another story. One time she got a ride request way out in the boonies. It was somewhere in the hills outside of Santa Barbara. She arrived to find some young people with a perfectly functioning automobile. The problem was the kids had taken too many drugs and were so high they couldn't find their way back. So they called for an Uber car to guide them out. Brilliant.

Uber Story 🚗 Uber Story 🚗 Uber Story

The Stranded Wine Tasters

In keeping with the *stranded* theme here is the story about how I started taking people on Uber wine tours via a service called **Uber Wine**. About three weeks after landing in Solvang I got a ride request quite some distance out of town. It was a good 40 minutes away, which in Santa Ynez Valley terms is the other side of the galaxy. I grabbed my gear and headed out.

The location was way out a road called **Foxen Canyon Road**.

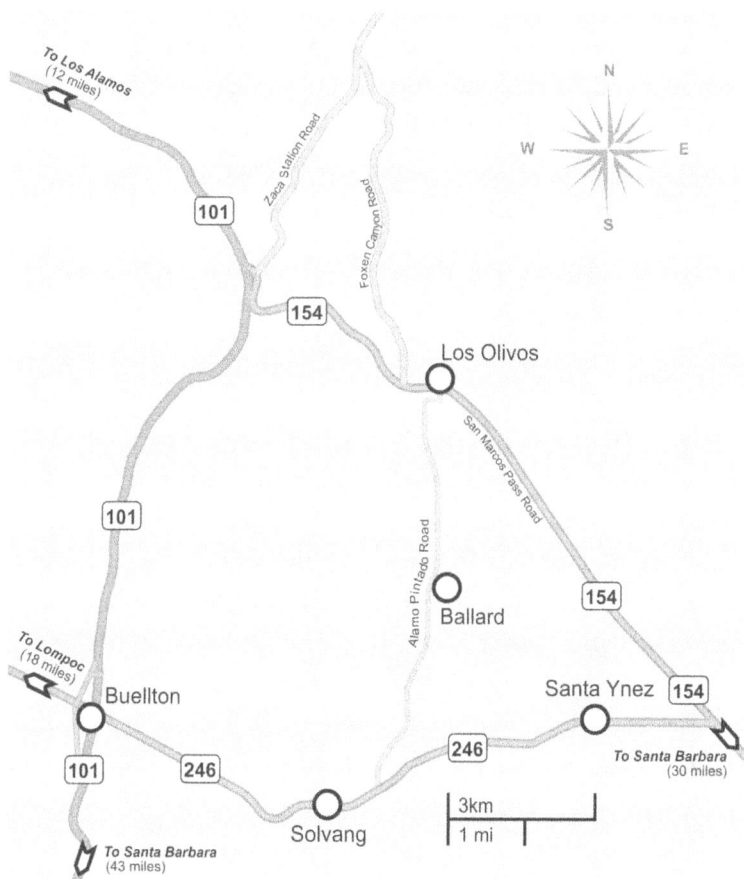

Map of Santa Ynez Valley

Foxen Canyon Road is just past the small town of Los Olivos at the north end of the valley. Once past Los Olivos the navigation assistant had me turn on to the road and the next thirty minutes were spent in paradise. Foxen Canyon is a classic country road winding through sparsely populated terrain. It

was all rolling hills, barbwire fences, corrals, dilapidated
barns... and grapevines. There are a number of wineries along
the way. Had no idea they even existed before then.

At some point cell reception is lost –not good for an Uber
driver- but the GPS stayed active and I finally found my fare at
a winery called Foxen Winery. Who knew? I pull into the
parking area and a lone woman rushes over to the car. Here is
how the conversation went:

Lady: "Hello. Are you the Uber driver who got a ride request for
a pickup at this winery?"

Uber James: "Yes."

Lady: "My name is Linda. I drive for Uber Wine. There is a
couple here who got stranded by another Uber driver. They
thought they had gotten an Uber Wine car, which means the
driver is supposed to wait and take the fare to the next tasting
room. But the guy said he couldn't stay. He dropped them in the
parking lot and took off."

Uber James: "Oh."

Lady: "Yeah, and the couple has been trying to get an Uber car
for a while now but the drivers keep cancelling when they see
how far away the pickup is. Let me go get them from inside.
They'll be really happy to see you."

They were. The relieved couple hopped in the car and we
started back to town. But what had happened here? Where did
Uber Linda come from? How did she get involved? Why was I
the only driver to fulfill the ride request?

Well it was happenstance, really. Uber Linda just happened to
be on an Uber Wine fare. Her passengers had come to Foxen –
which turns out to be a very popular winery- and Linda was

doing what Uber Wine drivers do..... wait for their fare in the parking lot... which is where she witnessed the whole thing go down with the stranded couple. I responded to the request because being young and naive I was responding to all requests. And as mentioned, it's a policy I adopted and try to stick to. Hey, people need rides. Our job as Uber drivers is to render the rides. Let's not overthink it. You get a request you take it. We're not splitting atoms here.

As it happens, taking this particular request altered the course of my Uber career in the valley. Seeing all those wineries made it finally sink in what the area was all about and where the fares were going to come from. I said to myself: *"It's the wine stupid!"* The following day I registered the car for Uber Wine.

Note: At the time of this writing the Uber Wine service is only available in two counties in the nation; Santa Barbara county, CA and adjacent San Luis Obispo County.

Uber Story   🚗   Uber Story   🚗   Uber Story

Uber James' First Wine Fare

It took a few weeks but the Prius finally started showing up on the rider app under both Uber X and Uber Wine. Great. Part of the reasoning behind signing up for Uber Wine was to get back out to Foxen Canyon Road. It's beautiful country and I wanted to see more of it. That turned out to be a good strategy because as it happens most of the Uber Wine requests that came through were from people who wanted to visit the wineries on Foxen Canyon. This is where people really needed Uber because once you're out there the odds of getting another ride slim considerably the further out you go. Partly due to driver's reluctance to make the journey and partly due to crappy cellular phone reception. Keep in mind that the main difference between regular Uber and Uber Wine is that the driver agrees to stay with the fare until released. The only other difference is that the waiting charge, which in this locale is 22 cents a minute, jumps to 29 cents for Uber Wine. The mileage charge of $1.25 per mile remains the same.

Taking groups on Uber Wine tours was fun and profitable. I say "tour" to distinguish the type of fare, but there is no actual guided tour. Uber Wine does not require drivers to have any knowledge of wine whatsoever, and fares seem to intuitively know that. If they want an actual tour of the wineries and a driver who can contrast the difference between the 2013 Melville Pinot Noir and the 2013 Alma Rosa Pinot Noir, given they are the same vintage and the grapes are from the same region, then they should be hiring one of the long established and far more expensive wine tour services. But yes, just as Uber has disrupted the taxicab industry it is now doing the same to the wine tour industry in California.

Anyway my very first wine fare was to.... you guessed it... Foxen Canyon. There was some initial paranoia as to whether the passengers were expecting me to actually **know** anything about wine. I knew a little. I've certainly drunk plenty of it. In my younger days there were a number of excursions to the northern California Napa and Sonoma wine regions. But my current wine knowledge is limited to knowing where in Trader Joe's the cases of Two-Buck Chuck are located (*for years the West Coast Trader Joe's grocery chain has sold a few common varieties of Charles Shaw wine for $2 a bottle. Even though the price was eventually raised to $2.50, the Two-Buck Chuck moniker remains. The Chardonnay once won a blind tasting, so my apologies only stretch so far*).

As it turned out there were no issues with my wine knowledge. *All that first wine fare cared about was that the driver knew the way to the next tasting room and would be there when they came out.* These people were pros. They were out of L.A. They came to the valley quite often. They had money, and were coming out of the wineries with cases of wine under their arms. So it actually turned out that the passing of wine knowledge was from *them* to *me*. But I couldn't assume that everyone getting in the car for a wine tour were going to be as sophisticated as these folks. There was not only a need to get up to speed on navigating the area and learn of the hotspots, the good eateries, the watering holes, etc.... it seemed wise to learn a bit about the wines of the region. There are quite a number of varietals grown in the numerous and varied micro-climates in and around the valley so I always tuned into my fare's reaction to the tasting they had just attended.

Note: If you're not wine savvy the term 'varietal' simply refers to a specific kind -or variety- of grape, like Chardonnay or Pinot Noir. Traditional French wines are labeled based on the region the grape is from —such as Beaujolais- whereas American wines are labeled by the grape the wine is made from. A wine made predominantly from a single grape (75% or more) is termed a varietal. Conversely, wines made from several varietals are termed 'blends'.

My current fare was delighted to give me their opinion on the wine they had just tasted. All the fares were. That was the key to coming up to speed quickly. I grilled my fares. I downright interrogated them as to what their opinions were on the wine, the restaurants... anything to do with the valley. *And everyone was happy to comply.* I was unable to taste the wine so instead lived vicariously off my passengers. There were certain restaurants I never made it into, but my fares had given me blow by blow descriptions that could be passed on to the next fare.

If a local stepped into the car it was even better. They were able to color in the history of the valley. For example I learned from one guy that Santa Ynez had only dirt roads just a few decades ago. A Chumash gentleman had an aunt that used to work in the food service area of the Indian casino and make the goat cheese and fry bread served to the gamblers.

For the next several weeks my mind was like a sponge, absorbing every tidbit of valley knowledge it could get its hands on. It was a fun exercise. I recall one afternoon in particular when an Uber Wine fare request came in... I recognized the Solvang motel they were requesting from, drove to their location sans navigation and retrieved them. Once tucked into the car they announced:

Passenger: "Hi! We want to go to Lincort, then to Foxen Shack, because it closes early. Then to Kholer, then to Andrew Murray."

Uber James: "Not a problem."

It was a random list of wineries starting in Solvang, running half way down Foxen Canyon Road, and then back again to the mouth of Foxen Canyon. I knew the locations by heart. On that day it felt like the homework was paying off.

That trip went well. The fare -who routinely made the excursion from L.A.- were enjoying themselves. At the end of the day the couple slipped me a $40 tip on a $150 fare. So yes, I'm pretty sure that was a 5-star ride. And of course it wasn't just about the stars. Getting stars is a fun game that was certainly a bit of an obsession. But that's not what's paramount during the trip. The idea is that the fare has a great time. What I had

POINT A TO POINT B 63

learned is that these wine tours were not simply about taking the fare from point A to point B. The driver, even more than with regular fares, is included in the adventure. In an Uber car there's no partition separating driver and passengers. No window that the fare can slide closed. It's not a limousine ride. It's not an anonymous cab ride. *On an Uber Wine excursion the driver is part of the experience.* I observed that by being in a good mood, smiling, interacting, asking questions... the tasters were sort of able to carry the experience they had had in the tasting room right into the car and onto the next winery.

Uber Story 🚗 Uber Story 🚗 Uber Story

The Three Happy Nurses

Pop quiz: How fast do people get plastered when wine tasting?

Well the short answer is, it varies. Some folks really meter themselves. They drink slowly... they nibble on food. The best "metered" fare I ever had –in turns of the fare never appearing intoxicated whatsoever- was a mother and daughter who were up for the weekend to celebrate the daughter's birthday. The ladies hit half a dozen wineries. I kept waiting for the tell-tale signs but they never came. The girls maintained perfectly throughout the day, their mood never changing a whit.

Others just go for it. On that end of the spectrum I recall a fare of three lovely young ladies. They were nurses in the same hospital that had finagled a couple of days off to shoot up to wine country and cut loose. Metering was not a concern. They had me take them out Foxen Canyon Road, sipping liberally all the way to Foxen Winery. On the return trip the car was all about laughing girls, somewhere past tipsy, but never unladylike. We drove over a tarantula on the way back. We didn't *hit* the creature. The car literally drove over it as it was crossing the road. The girls hadn't seen it so I asked them if they wanted to go back. "YES YES!" came the reply. We reversed course and found it still crossing the road. One of the girls popped out of the car with her camera, ran right up to the tarantula, stooped down and started taking pictures inches away. NO FEAR! Guess she hadn't seen Dr. No.

Tarantula on Foxen Canyon Rd.

The nurses cut me loose at Los Olivos while they explored the town on foot. I happened to get their ride request later on when everything was shutting down for the day. I found the girls pouring themselves out of the last tasting room, one of them laughing and struggling to hold onto a case of wine, another trying to help but really wasn't. Yeah, they were fully lit at this point.

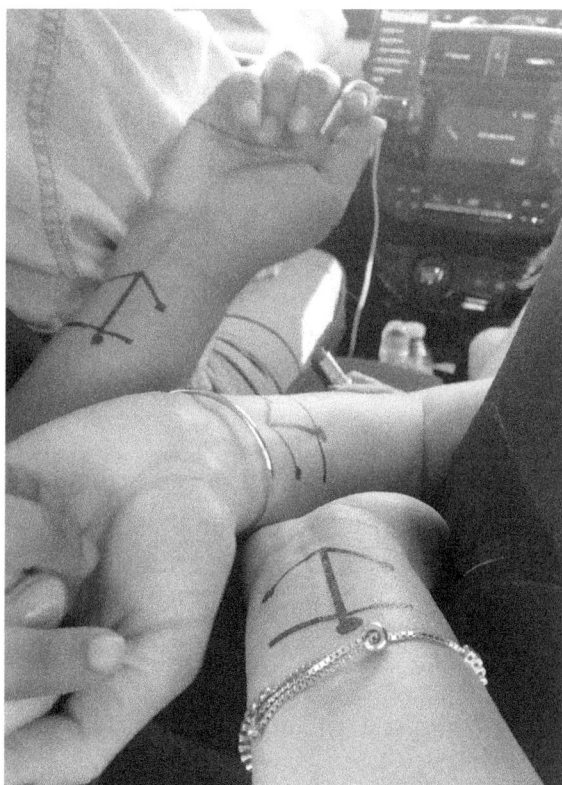

These temporary tattoos are the crest of the last visited winery.

But see? This is as bad as "the other end of the spectrum" got on wine tours. The nurses had a great day, no one got out of control, and I got to drive three cute girls around. What's not to love?

After the first Uber Wine fare I had the idea to put together some music playlists geared to the intoxication level of the passengers. I'd take measure of the fare's happy level after each tasting and engage the corresponding playlist.

There was a pre-tasting play list as well as post-tasting play lists levels I through IV. The pre-tasting list consisted of what might be characterized as really really good elevator music. It was a set-the-mood-but-don't-interrupt motif. A little jazz from Spyro Gyra and Danny Gatton. A touch of Bossa Nova in the form of The Girl from Ipanema. A few of Van Morrison's more melodic cuts. Some World Music from Putumayo. This would get us to the first winery with room to spare. From there each playlist kicked it up a notch until at level IV it was all out bang-your-head sing-at-the-top-of-your-lungs rock-and-roll.

Some tasters would emerge from their first testing ready for level I or II. For others it was straight to level IV. I had a fare one time who never got past the pre-tasting set. Others skipped the pre-tasting set altogether as they were already in the mood. Everybody's different.

Uber Story   🚗   Uber Story   🚗   Uber Story

Next Stop… The Twilight Zone

One day the driver app lit up for an Uber Wine pickup. The pickup address was a restaurant in downtown Solvang about three blocks from my motel. In a minute the Prius was parked in front and out comes one of the first couples I had done an Uber Wine tour with. It had been out Foxen Canyon Road, and that is where they wanted to go that day. I drove the fare around to several wineries. The couple is having its usual good time. They emerge from one of the wineries with a package containing a pair of freshly purchased wine glasses and stash the box in the back seat.

Later we come out of Foxen Canyon and go into Los Olivos. The couple decides to turn me loose and walk the tasting rooms. When getting out of the car the man notices the wine glasses. "Darn. We've got these glasses." I interject that I'd be happy to drop the box at their hotel. They accept the offer with thanks. I know they're staying at 'The Landsby' but confirm. The reply comes back, "Yes, The Landsby." We say our good-byes and I go back ONLINE.

Sometime later that day I'm in Solvang. I park at The Landsby hotel and run in with the box containing the glasses. I approach the front desk and ask the clerk if he can take possession of the box until the couple returns. The clerk asks for their last name and the room number. There is a delay while he looks up the name. Then more delay.

Clerk: *"I'm sorry sir there is no one registered by that name."*

Uber James: *"Are you sure?"*

Clerk: *"Yes. I'm looking again and these people are not registered here."*

Uber James: *"Under that room number"?*

Clerk: *"Not in any room."*

I thank the man and leave. This is strange. I knew I had the right hotel. The people were in the car two hours ago. They were real. They were in Solvang that day. If they had checked out early would the clerk not have seen that? It just didn't make sense. I flash on all the movies I've ever seen where people mysteriously disappear: The Girl with the Dragon Tattoo; Dangerous Crossing; A Star Trek episode called 'Remember Me'.

Finally I write the whole thing off to my sometimes faulty memory. Somehow I got the hotel wrong, and the couple would get in touch upon returning to their actual hotel and finding that the glasses not been dropped off.

No calls come in that night. No calls the next day. In fact they never did call. They didn't seem the type to make a purchase like that and then just let it go. The woman especially was on it. Very organized. Very specific about what she liked and didn't like. The whole wine tour had been thought out before they ever got in the car. These were not haphazard folks. If they bought two beautifully inscribed wine glasses they intended to take them home. Yet, I am still in possession of that pair of glasses. Weeks after this incident I had a thought to send them a message through Uber. I reported that the fare left an item in the car. Never got a reply.

Whenever strange things like this happen it brings to mind the theory of parallel universes. Two adjacent dimensions with an identical Earth... only not quite. For example, have you ever had a conversation with someone, and later make reference to the conversation, only to find the other person has **no memory** of it. Perplexing things like that that make you scratch head in bewilderment. If scientists ever come up with evidence that people sometimes cross over from one dimension to another; like to the one where that conversation had not taken place, or where that couple couldn't make it up to wine country that weekend due to work, and thus no wine glasses were purchased... life would make a bit more sense.

The Prius Super-duper Uber car parked at the motel and ready for action

SEVEN
THE DAYS OF WINE AND RANCHING
A BRIEF HISTORY OF THE SANTA YNEZ VALLEY

Overview
Down Through the Ages
The Five Cities of the Santa Ynez Valley
Solvang
Santa Ynez
Chumash Casino
Los Olivos
Ballard
Bonus City – Los Alamos

"That was goooooo-ooood!"
- Andy Griffith

Because the Santa Ynez valley is such a unique place to drive an Uber car I want to tell you a little bit about it in this chapter. Stories recommence in the next chapter.

The Santa Ynez Valley is a remarkable setting on many levels. The key market for on-demand ride sharing is wine tasting. 75% of the people who got in the car during the day were there for the wine. But visitors come to the Santa Ynez Valley for many reasons. They come for the award winning restaurants. They come to see the quaint village of Solvang, full of Danish architecture, Danish food, and an array of pastry shops, chocolate shops and many other kinds of shops lining Copenhagen St. They come to camp at the huge RV center in Buellton. Those with an equestrian lilt come to ride horses at remote resorts. The brides and grooms flock to the valley to get married. The gamblers come to play the slots at the Chumash casino. Others come to see Mission Santa Inés or check out the Parks-Janeway Carriage House at the Santa Ynez Valley Historical Museum. And if you want to do a little detective work you may be able to find your way to the Solvang Vintage Motorcycle Museum (I never found it).

Down Through the Ages

The history of the Santa Ynez Valley tells like much of California history. Going waaaay back, the topography was formed by earthquake faults and volcanic activity stemming from two plates of the earth's crust rubbing up against each other near the coast. The resulting instability caused the land to rise, creating the five million year-old Santa Ynez Mountains and San Rafael Mountains that surround the valley. Steep mountain terrain, a National Forest, and vast tracks of surrounding agricultural and ranch lands conspire to set the Santa Ynez Valley apart from the rest of civilization.

Native Americans have lived around the valley for thousands of years (perhaps 13,000+ years). A sprawling tribe known as the Chumash (*bead maker* or *seashell people*) had some of their settlements around the valley. This local group of Chumash are known in today's terms as the 'Santa Ynez band of Chumash Indians'. Yes, they themselves employ the word "Indian" which kind of lets palefaces like me relax a bit and not be so concerned about accidentally employing an offensive word.

In 1769 the Spanish entered the valley, a marker denoting that the way of life for the Chumash was coming to an end. Later in 1804 Mission Santa Inés (Saint Agnes) was founded. It was one of 21 missions built in California ostensibly to convert and educate the natives, but had the unintended consequence of decimating the population from both natural and other causes.

Throughout the 1800s mission land was granted away, changing hands from the Native Americans to Spain, from Spain to Mexico, and finally falling into the hands of the United States. Large parcels of land were initially granted as *Rancheros*, which over time were broken up into smaller and smaller parcels as the population grew and the needs of the people inhabiting the land changed.

In terms of land use, the second half of the 19th century witnessed the blooming of **ranching** and **agriculture**. These two industries form the backbone of land traditional agriculture since 1968. Tourism got a foothold in the valley after World War II when the village of Solvang focused on presenting the town with an enhanced Danish motif. Indian gaming commenced in the 1990s. Release of the darkish comedy 'Sideways' in 2004 -which was set in the Santa Ynez Valley- flooded the area with wine tourists, which in turn spawned the growth of wine tasting establishments. Gourmet dining soon followed the wine tasters.

Today competing interests stand watch over the valley, attempting to balance the old world of agriculture and ranching with the new world of tourism and gaming.

The Five Cities of the Santa Ynez Valley

There are five towns encircling the valley. Each township is dramatically different from the others. Four of the locations form a sort of triangle, with Hwy 101 and Hwy 154 forming the west and east legs respectively, and Hwy 246 forming the third leg. The towns are a scant few miles apart from each other, with no more than a 10 minute drive from one to another.

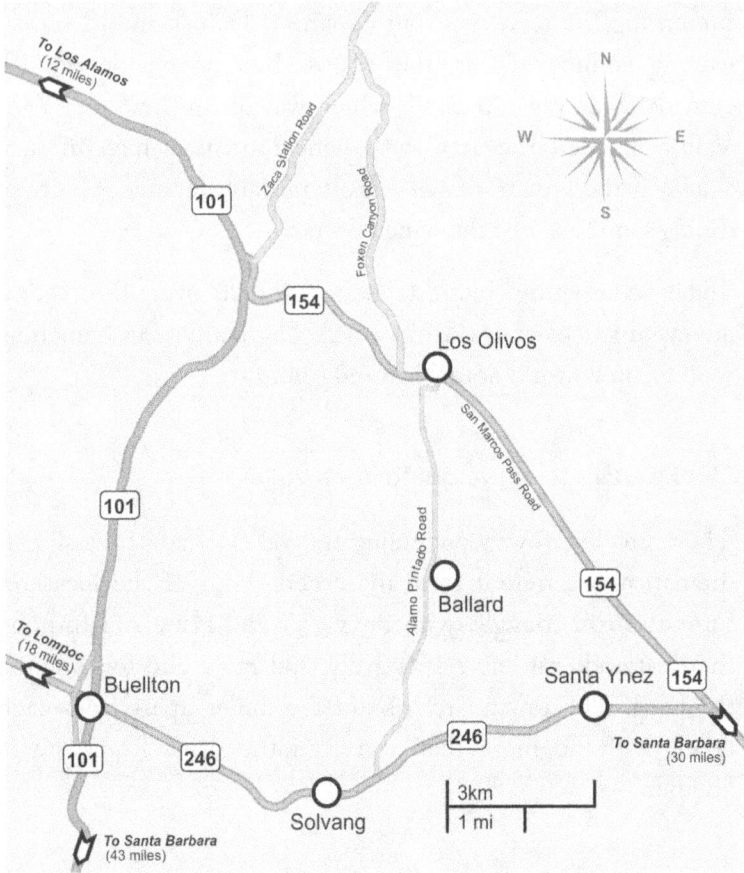

Map of Santa Ynez Valley

Buellton

Buellton is often thought of as a freeway stop because it is
located adjacent to the main highway running past the valley;
State Route 101. All the fast food is here, and *only* here. In
Buellton you'll find gas stations, major name hotels, an RV
park, and one major grocery store chain. To give you an idea
how small a civilization exists here, I was unable to buy a bath

towel anywhere in the valley. The Rite Aid store next to Albertson's in Buellton carried towels in the summer only, and this was September.

But don't judge this book by its cover. There are some great places to eat and drink in Buellton. Two favorites of mine are Industrial Eats (a MUST visit), and an authentic whole-in-the-wall Mexican place called El Sitio. For breakfast you can't beat Paula's Pancake House. For drinking, the Firestone Brewery and the Figueroa Mountain Brewery are popular Uber destinations. The steakhouse Hitching Post II, made famous by its inclusion in the film Sideways, lives on the edge of Buellton. If you love hamburgers and find yourself in The Hitching Post there's a secret item not on the menu: Over the weekend the kitchen saves the trimmings from the premium cuts of beef and on Monday-Wednesday nights they fresh grind the meat into giant hamburgers. You can almost split one between two normal people. Many other great eateries and drinking establishments can be found in Buellton as well.

Two Quick Uber Stories

The first time I went in to the Hitching post to try out the specialty burger there were two locals in a nearby corner enjoying themselves. They were friendly and when I said hello I learned that one of the pair, a woman, was a winemaker. She would be the first of several wine makers whose acquaintance I'd be fortunate enough to make, and their stories can be found in this book. The couple was drinking wine. I smiled over and told them if they had instead been drinking martinis I would tell them a martini joke. They wanted to hear it anyway. Would you like to hear it? *What does a martini and a woman's breasts have in common? ... One's not enough and three's too many.*

Second story: I picked up a fare from Firestone Brewery one time that was two guys who had flown out from back east and were using Uber to work their way up the California coast, hitting every brewery along the way. Hilarious, and perhaps one for the Guinness Book of World Records.

Solvang

Many people coming to the area are headed to Solvang. If I was trapped in one valley town for a week... no car... no Uber... I would probably stay in Solvang. Reason being, there's a little bit of everything here; accommodations, great restaurants, shops, wine tasting, events, and a particularly good grocery store. The downtown area is only a few blocks long, making it perfect to canvas on foot, days or evenings (there's virtually no crime). Or if you prefer, rent a 4-wheel bicycle or take a tour in a horse-drawn carriage.

Based on my Uber experience a significant number of tourists use Solvang as a base of operations to explore the valley. There are a number of hotels and motels that facilitate this. One standout hotel for wine tasters is the Hadsten House Inn and Spa. The spa is nice, but the real attraction is the coupon sheet each guest receives for free wine tasting, thanks to the deals the proprietors have made with local wineries. It's a full page long, and they don't jack up the price of the rooms to pull this off. Conversely if you're on a budget the nearby Viking Motel is a clean comfortable place to stay, and you can get to most anywhere in town on foot.

The nice thing about driving for Uber is that I got to see lots of nooks and crannies around the valley. One of the most singularly amazing finds was the Alisal Guest Ranch & Resort on the outskirts of Solvang. The resort is a few miles south of town, reachable by an old country road. The setting is idyllic. It's like something you'd see in a movie. Serene beauty. Food. Golf. Horseback riding. Simply entering the grounds brings about a sense of calm and relaxation. It's an amazing place.

Food-wise you can't go wrong in Solvang. There are many fine restaurants; some easily visible, some hidden away on side streets. Whether it's a gourmet sandwich at Panino, a bowl of premium chili at CHOMP Burgers, an Italian pizza at Cecco trattoria, or Danish Ebelskievers at The Red Viking it's all good. There's a Vietnamese restaurant called Pho 805 that serves the best chicken wings I've ever tasted. For those who can't resist a sweet dessert treat you need to go to the Succulent Café. Walk up to the take-out counter and look for the *pecan bacon desert squares* to the left. Buy one and prepare to die and go to heaven.

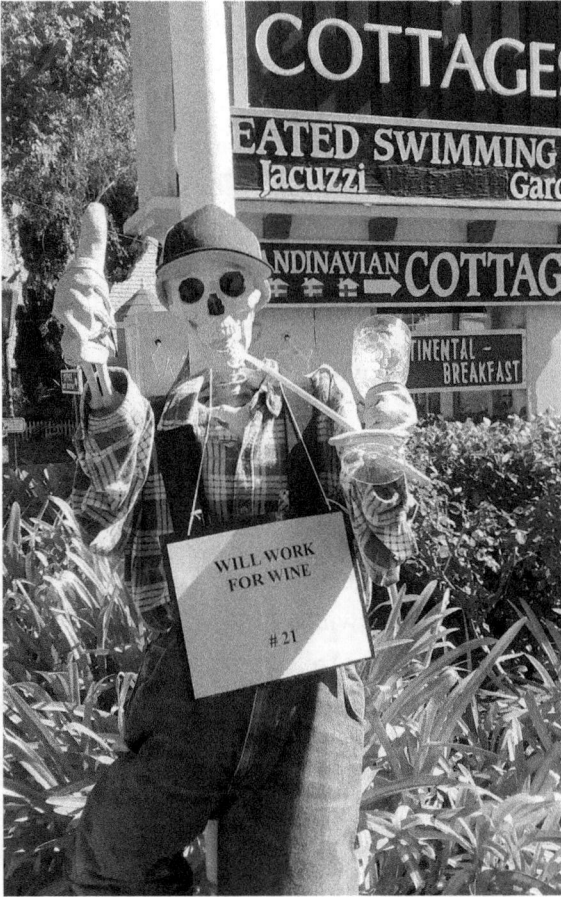

Halloween is a big deal in Solvang

The Final Frontier

At the east end of Solvang there is a great grocery store called
New Frontiers Natural Marketplace. For years New Frontiers
was a small west coast chain of natural food stores. I say *was*
because all the stores have closed except the one in Solvang.

The New Frontiers store in Solvang is the last of its namesake. They have refused to sell out to the larger chains. The employees refer to the store as 'The Final Frontier'. I told them they should have t-shirts.

Santa Ynez

Santa Ynez is the town that most represents the ranching heritage of the valley. The far flung unincorporated township boasts the highest concentration of horse ranches, where old and new money have staked out a corner of the world to live life on its own terms. This is salt-of-the-earth "Ronald Regan country." The ex-President's ranch *Rancho del Cielo* (Heaven Ranch) is located on a hilltop with Santa Ynez.

One picture is indeed worth a thousand words. All four sides of the main downtown intersection have these embedded horseshoes.

This tiny town may well sport the highest concentration of outstanding restaurants per square foot. There's also a few fine Inns located here, such as the Santa Ynez Inn and the ForFriends Inn. There's a little wine tasting, and several points of interest worth visiting such as the Santa Ynez Valley Historical Museum & Parks-Janeway Carriage House.

But the big draw is that the notably small downtown area is host to a range of fine dining establishments (no tie required). I took more people on Uber rides to these restaurants than perhaps any others in the valley. Mexican food is covered more than adequately by Dos Carlitos. Across the street is The Brothers Restaurant at the Red Barn. Fares rave about the steaks, and I can testify they serve a terrific burger with all the fixings. A block down the street finds the restaurant I probably took more fares to than any other: SY Kitchen. People love this Italian restaurant. Although I never imbibed while driving Uber, rumor has it they build a mean Old Fashioned at the bar.

Around the corner from SY Kitchen lies Trattoria Grappolo, which some Italians (from Italy) told me serves the most authentic Italian food around. Very popular. Several other gems in this town as well, such as the CRUDO bar at the 'Eleven Wine Lounge'.

My personal favorite restaurant in Santa Ynez is the Baker's Table. They have a variety of baked goods and some breakfast and lunch items. First time in I bought a handful of cookies and took them back to the motel. My mind was blown. The textures and subtle levels of flavor in the cookies was completely unexpected. I was back the next day buying more, and the owner, Amy, was there. I wanted to describe how good the cookies were and they only way I could articulate the experience was to tell her "It's like eating poetry." Big Smile back from Amy.

Chumash Casino Resort

The tallest building in Santa Ynez, and in the entire valley for that matter, is the Chumash Casino. I'll tell you, there is a book full of storytelling about these Native Americans alone, but for now here's a few highlights. The 14 story casino building sits on Native American soil -the 127 acre Chumash Reservation- and houses a Nevada style casino, showrooms booked with a constant stream of special events, restaurants, and of course accommodations.

Back view of 14-story Chumash Casino

That's now. Twenty years ago, when I visited the casino for the first time on a day trip from Santa Barbara, all that was there was a canvas covered Quonset hut (a half-circle metal framed building). Early on, the makeshift building was used for bingo. Slot machines and blackjack tables were later added. To play blackjack one had to ante up 50 cents per hand. This went to the house.

Tacked on to the back of the Quonset hut was another tent. Inside that tent was the food service, where chickens and goats occupied a portion of the real estate. The chickens provided fresh eggs for omelets, and the goats provided the milk used to make a special cheese that's eaten with the homemade Chumash fry bread. I've had Chumash Indians as Uber fares who recall those days and speak with fond memories of the fry bread.

Today the 24/7 casino draws in the wine tasters, the Solvang tourists, folks from surrounding communities such as Santa Barbara, and in fact from everywhere. The interior of this modern casino is indistinguishable from its Reno counterparts. The Chumash took their lessons from the pros. Gone are the ante trays from the old blackjack tables. Clearly they figured out that there is plenty of profits for the house just winning straight hands of blackjack. Between a variety of table games, slots, bingo, and all the other profitable businesses within the building, the Santa Ynez band of the Chumash have literally gone from rags to riches. In two decades these people have advanced from abject poverty to one of the wealthiest groups in the valley. I was told that every person with a threshold percent of Chumash blood gets a piece of the casino action in the form of a monthly stipend. The tribe owns other land, hotels, and restaurants around the valley. And who can blame them?

The Best Grocery Store in the Whole World

There is an amazing grocery store in Santa Ynez called El Rancho Market. Indeed the term "marketplace" fits better than *grocery store*, because they have everything under the sun. Take a look:

- Coffee bar
- Juice bar
- Burrito / taco bar
- Sushi bar
- Soup bar
- Breakfast bar
- Lunch bar
- Full service deli

- Hot and cold prepared meals
- Bakery
- BBQ
- Huge selection of wine
- Booth and patio seating outside
- And, it's a grocery store too!

I would joke with my fares that it seemed worth moving to Santa Ynez just to be able to shop at this store every day. If there is an El Rancho location in heaven then I'll be set when I pass on. Come to think of it perhaps there should be one in all three locations... just in case.

Los Olivos

Los Olivos (the olives) is a town of historical significance. It was a stage coach stop in the late 1800's. The narrow gauge railroad coming down from Los Alamos terminated at Mattie's Tavern in Los Olivos where disembarking passengers would board a stage coach that took them over the treacherous San Marcos pass and down into Santa Barbara, with an interim stop at the Cold Spring Tavern near the pass. Today, Mattie's Tavern and Cold Springs Tavern still exist, and the mostly 2-lane San Marcos pass is still treacherous.

Los Olivos has two renowned restaurants that were frequent targets of my Uber passengers: Wine Merchant Café and Sides Hardware. Yes, that's the name of the latter establishment. It's actually 'Sides Hardware and Shoes; a Brothers Restaurant.' What kind of a way is that to name a restaurant? Recall the steakhouse mentioned earlier in Santa Ynez called 'The

Brothers Restaurant at the Red Barn'. It's the same brothers. Matt and Jeff Nichols. They have named both establishments with reference to each building's historical significance. The building in Santa Ynez was a barn, and the Los Olivos building was a hardware store run by a man named 'Sides' (and apparently he sold shoes there too).

But to get to the heart of the matter Los Olivos is the go-to destination for wine tasting. Tasting rooms are nearly elbow to elbow on each single block extending from the town center. This is a peaceful locale where you can park your car and sip your wine at any of perhaps two dozen tasting rooms, easily sauntering from one to the next.

Ballard

Ballard is the smallest township, and unlike the other three it's located in the interior of the triangle. When I was visiting all that was up and running was the lovely Ballard Inn & Restaurant. This is where you stay if you're seeking a quiet respite in the valley. Ballard is quite separated from the micro-civilizations in all directions, yet you're 10-15 minutes from accessing any of it again. There's also a number of Airbnb cubby holes in the area surrounding Ballard.

Bonus City: Los Alamos

Less than 15 minutes north of Los Olivos lies the semi-isolated yet up and coming wine country town of Los Alamos (the cottonwood trees). The Seven-block long town has become known for its fantastic array of eating establishments. I haven't had the chance to eat there yet, but an Uber passenger in the know ranked the 1880 Union Hotel (a stage coach stop in its day) as comparable to a high-end Los Angeles restaurant. At the north end of town lies Full of Life Flatbread. I'm told their pizza alone is worth the drive. The main drag of this western motif town is littered with interesting eating spots, motels, wine tasting, and other points of interest. You'll be reading later about a local wine maker who grows his grapes in Los Alamos.

The 1880 hotel in Los Alamos. The stage to Santa Barbara stopped here.

EIGHT

UBER TALES FROM THE HEART

Uber Stories:

The Incredible Lightness of Beaming

JT Does Not Stand For Justine Timberlake

The Girl Who Came Upon Her Mojo in the Santa Ynez Valley

The Case of the Disappearing Fare

The 7959 Story

"Only a life lived for others is a life worthwhile."
- Albert Einstein

Uber Story   🚗   Uber Story   🚗   Uber Story

The Incredible Lightness of Beaming

There are a few experiences and memories from driving Uber that I wouldn't trade for anything. Case in point: One night the app lit up for a pickup at AJ Spurs, a steak house in Buellton. AJ's is a stone's throw from The Hitching Post II, the restaurant immortalized in the popular film 'Sideways'. AJ's, as with the Hitching Post, is always a source of happy and contented fares.

And that was the case with the large family that came through the doors of AJ's after getting signaled their Uber car was await-ing. There was mom, dad, at least three children, and some other odds and ends relatives or friends. It was enough people that they needed two Uber cars. I got mom and a bunch of kids. The children were perfect looking blondes. Any one of their faces could be smiling at you from within a picture fame at Walgreens. As the father walked by me on his way to the second car he playfully said *"Don't worry if you lose them on the way to the campground."* There was a sort of warm presence to the group. The adults were full of happy juice and animal protein, and the kids were delighted about some takeaway presents from AJ's. What was that? Yes, apparently there is a toy chest in the restaurant and they actually let kids take some of the toys home.

As we pull out of the driveway the younglings are describing their cool presents to me. Their excitement about the toys begets an idea. The family is camping at the Flying Flags RV Park about a mile away. I think about my stash of "Boogie-lights" under the seat. Boogie-lights are micro keychain flashlights I market at a few gift shops in Big Sur. I keep a handful in the car and give them out under various circumstances. A favorite handout spot is the drive-through lane at fast food joints. If someone renders splendid service I hand 'em a boogie-light and watch their face light up. People intrinsically love flashlights, which of course is a core staple when camping. Even "RV" camping.

So outloud I say "Those are some pretty nice toys. But I'll tell you what. I think I can top that." I look over at mom in the front seat, asking permission with an expectant look on my face. She smiles and nods yes, probably curious what the heck this Uber driver is capable of producing on the *spur* of the moment. The kid's attention is piqued. They accept the challenge. We pull into the RV Park and up to the family's site. Everybody piles out and I reach under my seat for the tin full of flashlights. The kids shoot around the back of the car and line up in front of me. I don't know how it worked out but the young man from the back seat is not present. Standing in front of me though are the two girls, apparently sisters. I would put their ages and five and eight.

I pull out a Boogie-light and fire it up. The girls now have an inkling of what's in store for them. These are especially bright flashlights for their size and will blind you for a moment if looked at directly. I hand the taller girl the light, asserting how you just *have* to have a flashlight when you go camping. She grabs the light and smiles. Then I turn on a second light and hand it to the five year old. The little one's amazed reaction was priceless. She took hold of her light, stared at it for a moment, then looked up at me. Huge smile. She acted as thought I had gifted her the sun, and shone like it. She makes direct eye contact with me, as an adult would, but doesn't say a word. This tiny creature just beams this enormous bouquet of gratitude my way.

It was a surreal moment. I'd never seen such a joyful face. For a second I thought to myself maybe that's just how these particular kids react to things, but during this display her mom reached her arm around me and gave a squeeze. That was the signal it *was* an unusual event. The Boogie-lights clearly had won first prize in the toy competition. The children ran off in delight, lighting up everything in the campsite with their newly acquired playthings.

And that was that. Like so many Uber fares, we said goodbye and went on with our own lives.

The Infamous Big Sur Boogielight

Uber Story   🚗   Uber Story   🚗   Uber Story

JT Does Not Stand For Justine Timberlake

This is a bitter sweet tale. On an Uber Wine tour my fare stopped at Tres Hermanes Winery along Foxen Canyon Road. The winery is adjacent to the highway. As we pull into the driveway, dead ahead lies an old red barn with the giant initials JT emblazoned above the doors. One of the passengers jokes that the winery must be owned by Justine Timberlake and the others giggle a bit. We come to a stop at the actual tasting room to the right of the barn and the passengers disembark to complete their assigned mission. I pull the car to the other end of the parking area and bring the Prius to rest under a tree by the fence bordering the road.

I'm sitting in the car enjoying a beverage and snack, listening to music and contemplating the nature of the universe when two bicyclists appear on the horizon. As the cyclers approach the winery they slow at the driveway and one of the pair, a male in his 40's, breaks off and continues into the parking lot of the winery, while the female rests at the entrance. The gentleman glides right up to the barn, swings the bike parallel to the doors, and comes to a halt directly under the JT initials.

My curiosity is piqued. Why did the man break off from the other rider? Why did he enter the property? Are they working up to a tasting? It does happen. No. The man simply stayed right there in front of the barn. He had lowered his head, seemingly resting. As it happens the wall of the barn was providing one of the few shady spots in the area. So that made sense. He was just getting out of the heat of the day for a bit. The guy was there for a quite a while however, and I started to wonder if maybe he had a touch of heat exhaustion or was possibly depleted of electrolytes. It was a warm day and Foxen Canyon is a long road. Finally the man pulled himself fully on to his bicycle and began peddling back toward the entrance to rejoin his partner.

I was a bit concerned. Did they need water? We were in the middle of nearly nowhere and cell reception is poor. I had enough water for half the valley in the back of the Prius, and as it happens a handy-dandy first aid kit with a few packets of electrolyte powder. So as the bicycles passed by I waved the guy over. He complied. I told him of my stash of H2O and minerals and that he was certainly welcome to them. He said "No, I'm OK. What it is..."

I'm smiling as he talks. He reveals that his reason for stopping at the barn is that he had lost his son in a car accident a few years before. My smile turns to anguish and I sort of excuse myself. He smiles, brushes the small faux pa aside, and continues. The JT on the barn matched his son's initials. He had bicycled the road before losing his son and knew of the giant letters attached to that barn. Since then he makes the pilgrimage every year and stops at the barn in remembrance.

I thanked him for sharing his story. He certainly didn't have to. But he seemed at peace with it all. Then off the two riders went down Foxen Canyon Road.

Note: What exactly are those initials doing there? That was the brand for when the land was used to run cattle a mere generation ago. The children switched over to growing grapes. Another sign of the changing face of the Santa Ynez Valley.

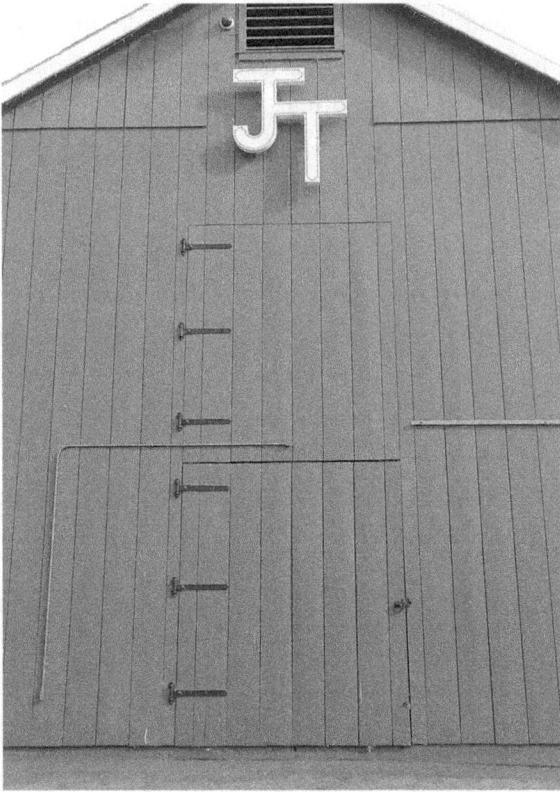

JT Barn

Uber Story   🚗   Uber Story   🚗   Uber Story

The Girl Who Came Upon Her Mojo
in the Santa Ynez Valley

I picked up a fare one evening at a popular wine tasting bar in Solvang. The place had just closed and my passenger turned out to be an employee needing a ride home. It was a striking young blonde woman. She sat in the back seat and as it happens was in a talkative mood. We conversed the entire way to her ranch in Santa Ynez. She told me the story of how she had reclaimed her life by moving to the valley.

It was a simple story really. And a familiar one. The girl had spent much of her twenties trying out different careers, looking for something that would satisfy her. She had worked in hotel management ... tried out various gigs in L.A., Vegas, and New York... but nothing resonated. She was not leading a fulfilling life.

A common story, yes. But what is perhaps less common is that this woman did something about it. She dropped out, did some soul searching, and ended up seeking out an entirely different lifestyle. Which brought her to the Santa Ynez Valley. Which found her a home at a Santa Ynez ranch. Which filled her life full of horses and pigs and goats and chickens. Not to mention a passel of dogs and an organic garden.

Had the young lady found her bliss? All I can say is that the woman was happy every time I encountered her in future Uber rides.

Uber Story   🚗   Uber Story   🚗   Uber Story

The Case of the Disappearing Fare

One night a ride request comes in for a pickup at a residence in Santa Ynez. This usually meant a local wanting a ride or a tourist staying at an Airbnb. In this case it was just a local needing a ride to the grocery store. I drove him the two miles or so to El Rancho Market. The fare exited the car and I waited while he did his shopping.

Some time goes by. Maybe 10 minutes. Then some more time. I

wasn't looking at my watch but my uber senses were informing me that something was not right with this picture. The meter was running on the Uber ride. The gentleman had reluctantly agreed to allow that or he would have had to cut me loose and call for another car when done shopping. I therefore assumed he was on a budget and would not be loitering in the market.

More time goes by. I get out of the car, meander over to the font of the store and peer through the windows and down the aisles. The fare is not visible. So now the choice was to either go back and wait in the car, or investigate further. I really did feel something was amiss. Not that there was anything really *wrong*. Just that something was out of place.

So I went into the store and performed a more thorough recon. It's not a huge store so it didn't take long. Extra time was spent looking down the aisles twice to account for the fact that the shopper might have been exactly in-between two aisles as I scanned each one from the other end. If you've ever looked for someone in a grocery store you know what I mean. But I couldn't find him. He wasn't in the deli, he wasn't in produce, he wasn't down any of the main aisles... he just wasn't. The dude just wasn't there.

I went back to the car. Had he slipped by me? Was he waiting in the car? No. I turn and look back into the store. There he is! He's checking out. And something *was* wrong. The checkout process was not proceeding normally. How did I know? Nobody was moving. The clerk wasn't ringing up grocery items or packing them in a bag. My fare wasn't reaching in his pocket or sliding a credit card. Nor was he hovering over the credit card scanner waiting for the charge to process. None of that typical movement was occurring. It was like a stand-off. Was the machine broken?

I had a feeling that the problem lay with my fare. I went back into the store and right up to the checkstand, just in time to hear the clerk say "What would you like to take back?"

Uh huh! He doesn't have enough money to pay for his groceries. So no, it wasn't the end of the world, but the thing is, even when prompted by the clerk to select which items he wanted to return the guy did not move. The poor fellow was just having a brain fart or something.

All this happens in a few moments. Again, everyone is just standing there. Shoppers are piling up behind my fare at what was the only checkstand open that late. No tempers are flaring but it's only a matter of seconds before the tension increases. In that instant I saw a solution to the problem. One that would instantly make the whole issue go away.

I walked up to the credit card terminal, pulled out my wallet, and slid my credit card through.

All better. The gentleman protested slightly but I begged him to let me help, with the cover story that I hadn't done my good deed for the day yet, and it was really *him* helping *me* out (which from a certain perspective is fully true). He relented. I don't know what the other people were thinking. The clerk knew me, but she didn't know the man was my Uber fare. The people in line knew even less. But the charge went through, the clerk handed the man his receipt, he grabbed his groceries and soon both the situation and the sliding glass doors of the store were behind us.

On the trip back the gentlemen of course offered to pay me back. The groceries had turned out to be only $18, so I told him not to worry about it (he seemed near broke). When he pushed it just a teeny bit I said to him something that a kind person who had once helped me out said... *"Pass it along."* He said he would.

The next day I saw a new passenger comment on my driver app. The man had posted what is easily the kindest compliment I received while driving in the valley. Thanks for that.

Uber Story   🚗   Uber Story   🚗   Uber Story

The 7959 Story

Here's another one. I picked up these two nice people one afternoon. It was a couple up from LA. They were members of this sort of boutique wine club. The wine clubs seem very popular with the aficionados, and of course with the wineries. Wine clubs facilitate sales, especially for hard-to-find vintages not available in stores. Marketing wine, like all consumer items, is all about distribution. There's probably more wine seeking shelf space than there is shelf space. Moreover, smaller wineries may not produce enough cases each year to satisfy the demand of a chain retailer. So how do such boutique wineries get their offerings to market? Enter the boutique wine club. That is what the 'Santa Ynez Valley Wine Club' -the destination of my fare today- is all about. Proprietors Gabe and Jen look for winemakers that produce no more than 1,000 cases per year, often far less. They assemble collections of wines and hold tastings for their limited membership. Today was a tasting exclusively for the couple in the back of the Prius. It was being held at a winery in Santa Ynez that is distinguished as being the first property in the valley to have grapevines planted back in 1968.

Surprisingly, the couple invited me to attend the tasting with them. Of course! I couldn't partake but there was a lot to learn regardless. The tasting was outdoors at an informal setting by a pond. The selection of the day occupied one side of the table and glasses for the tasters occupied the other. It was a warm sunny afternoon and we had some side entertainment in the form of a high-fashion photo shoot taking place a few yards away.

I forget the names of most of the offerings, except a selection with a label that had a drawing of a handgun placed near a rose. The obvious inference was that the winemaker was paying homage to the rock group Guns & Roses. The wine itself was a Rosé of course. There was one other bottle that distinguished itself with a label containing only the numbers '7959'. There was a tale to tell with regard to this particular wine, which Gabe indicated he would impart a bit later.

The tasting commenced, and while the two members enjoyed sips from the half dozen selections, Jen and Gabe gave us an education on the wines at hand as well as the particulars of winemaking in the Santa Ynez Valley. I noticed Gabe would use the word *fruit* quite a bit when referring to the grapes as opposed to just saying *grapes*. Not being a head-over-heels wine connoisseur I wasn't familiar with the term being used in that context. But I liked it. Fruit! *"The fruit is harvested from the vineyard and brought to the winery for processing." "We've seen some splendid fruit this year."* Like that. So, that's how the cool people do it, and if you were naïve like me you too can now be cool.

Later in the tasting the promised 7959 story was told. Gabe had actually made the wine himself. He had produced a small batch... his first effort... a Syrah. But what was the genesis of the label? Gabe's parents had migrated to America from Chili. Like many immigrants, his father had big plans for a successful career in the States. He was a well-educated man who had been an executive for an oil company in his fatherland.

But after settling in America Gabe's father was never able to kick start the career he was imagining. There was one headwind after another, and finally, in order to feed his family, Gabe's dad took a job as a bus driver. The driver's badge he was issued was numbered 7959.

The paychecks started rolling in and the family survived. The father however did not feel good about his lot. He mourned not achieving his career goals. In the meantime Gabe grew up, and thanks to all his father had provided was able to achieve a successful career in his own right.

The Santa Ynez Valley Wine Club is a success. It has 500 members with a cap of 550. The membership cap is due to the small production numbers of the wines that Gabe and Jen bring to market. When Gabe decided to try out winemaking himself he wanted to fashion a label that would pay tribute to his father. Thus the 7959 label for that 2011 Syrah.

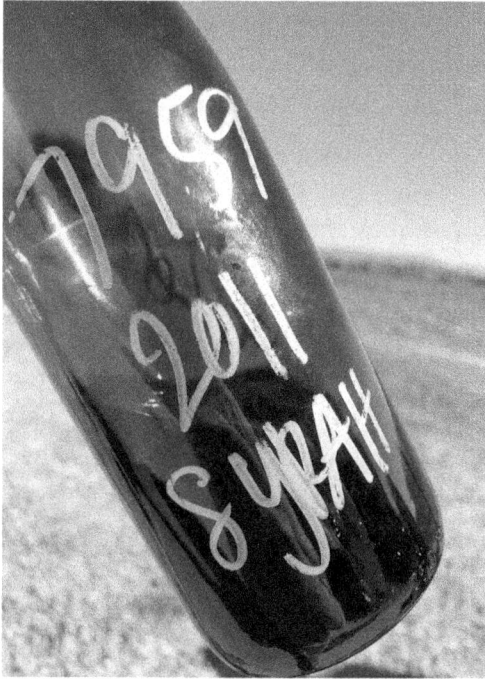

The "label" says it all

An Accidental Discovery

There was another aspect of the Uber driving experience that lends itself to the theme of this chapter. I was reminded of a fundamental lesson already known... and constantly forgotten. It is:

If you don't judge people they will love you

This was the feedback coming in as a result of the early adopted policy of trying to be nice to every fare even if there was something about them that put me off. The idea was to tolerate passengers regardless of their behavior, albeit drunk, arguing, loud, fat, creepy... or even slamming the door of my BRAND NEW CAR. Whatever. As long as the behavior didn't damage the Prius or interfere with my ability to safely pilot the car, forbearance was the guiding principle. Being somewhat of a temperament to *"not suffer fools gladly"*, effort was at times required.

But not only did this particular policy prevent any flare-ups from the back seat, people *noticed* they were being tolerated. Human beings know they're imperfect. And they know they can't do anything about it. God knows we've all tried. Our imperfections are like an open wound. We go about each day being judged and invalidated as people react to our wounds. And that opens the wound further. Just a little bit more each time.

So if a person is lucky enough to walk into a judgment-free zone... *they know it.*

Judgment-free zones are rare if you think about it. They can occur when hanging out with your pets. Pets don't judge. Same with small children. They haven't yet learned to judge. An elderly person who is full of a quality often described as *Grace* may provide a judgment-free environment. It's been known to happen in the early stages of romantic encounters. Wherever a judgment-free zone occurs it's treasured.

Without realizing it I had inadvertently created such a space in my Uber car. People often get on my nerves, but in the Prius, giving strangers 10 minute rides, 30 minute rides, even hours long rides, I had been able to suspend my judgment on the basis that it was a temporary relationship. Along with my totally unexpected, forest-fire induced summer vacation, I sort of took a vacation from judging the people taking rides in the Uber car.

Take for example the wine tasting couple in the previous story. The woman was a strong-willed person with definite opinions. As she sipped more and more wine she became more and more opinionated, sometimes dominating the conversation. Not in an extreme way. But enough to where she clearly had drawn criticism for such behavior in the past. How do I know? Because the next day I got the same couple as a fare. The lady was excited to have gotten 'Uber James' again and told me how much she appreciated being put up with the day before, which had included not only the tasting but driving the pair to dinner and then to their hotel. Her words of gratitude were backed up by a fat tip.

Tips in fact were a noticeable artifact of the judgment-free zone. Fares often tipped heavily. People would hand me fives... tens... twenties... sometimes more. I'm not young and "pretty" anymore so I don't really have any other way to account for the generosity. Happy juice played a role of course, but inebriation can push a person one way or the other, if you know what I mean.

Even when the Uber days came to an end, still present was this singular reminder of how much people appreciate not being judged. I am hopeful the remembrance of this lesson will continue and that I can carry it around in my back pocket in perpetuity. Only the most evolved of us can be provide a judgment-free zone to others at all times, but it helps to understand that when we judge others we are in fact judging ourselves. That sounds like a platitude, but in my experience the notion is true. If we can give *ourselves* a break, giving others a break becomes easier.

NINE

THE UBER UNCERTAINTY PRINCIPAL

Heisenberg vs Uber

Uber Driver Ratings Explained

Four Stars and You're Out

"I took a test in Existentialism.
I left all the answers blank and got 100."
- Woody Allen

Heisenberg vs Uber

People often inquire as to the inner workings of Uber. Many are surprised to learn that if all passengers rated their ride 4 stars (out of 5) the driver will soon be terminated. In this chapter I'd like to fill you in a bit on how Uber works from the driver's perspective. Feel free to skip if such trivia boars you.

The modern science of quantum mechanics tells us that we live in an uncertain world. Well, Duh! But now science seems to confirm what we humans already know. You've heard of the 'Heisenberg uncertainty principle'? Put simply it tells us that the reality of objects is so uncertain, simply observing an object can change it. It's the same with the thought experiment known as 'Schrödinger's cat'. A cat locked in a box and exposed to a randomly released poison is in an unknown state; maybe alive... maybe dead. The cat theoretically exists in both states simultaneously until someone opens the box and observes the cat. It's all about *probabilities*.

Uber has its own uncertainty principle. If you didn't understand any of the above it doesn't matter because Uber operates in its own universe. It's still a question of uncertainty and probabilities however. It boils down to the fact that an Uber driver knows little about his/her fare and destination until the passenger(s) is picked up. Nor can the driver be certain of the consequences of a variety of driving statistics tracked by Uber. The driver doesn't know the following:

Regarding Fares: When a ride request will come in

Regarding Fares: The destination of the fare (point B)

Regarding Fares: The number of people who will be getting into the vehicle

Regarding Fares: The disposition of those people

Regarding Fares: Whether or not the driver will be tipped

Regarding Fares: Any negative comment entered by a fare after the ride

Regarding Fares: What star rating other than 5 any of the fares gave you

Regarding Fares: What star rating 1-5 any *specific* fare gave you

Regarding Uber: how many ride requests a driver can ignore before it's a problem

Regarding Uber: how many ride cancellations a driver can have before it's a problem

To be fare –excuse me- fair, a driver *can* see the rider's star rating before the ride is accepted. If you happen to notice. The driver only has 30 seconds to accept an incoming request. Since a variety of things may be going on when the request comes in – phone in kitchen/driver in bathroom, phone screen off, another app is active, driver is on a phone call, etc.- you often don't have even that 30 seconds to scrutinize the request. Furthermore unless the driver app is in the foreground there is only one single beep (and a short vibration) announcing the request, instead of the continuous ping notification that occurs if the driver app is in the foreground and the screen is on (*This may be platform dependent. I was using Android).* So if the phone is in the driver's pocket he/she must... retrieve the phone, activate the lock screen, swipe to access the apps, switch the driver app to the foreground, examine and accept the incoming request.

All within 30 seconds. Now often that is enough time, especially if the driver is in the car and the phone is positioned in a nearby holder. But if for whatever reason the request expires, or the ride is cancelled afterwards (by driver *or* passenger), it is reflected in the driver's statistics. Not to mention the lost revenue.

Note: remember, these are all my experiences. Other drivers may/will have other experiences. Refer to the Preface.

Four Stars and You're Out

A couple of days into my driving career I was reading through some Uber support materials and learned that Uber fires drivers who don't consistently get an average rating close to 5-stars. What? Yes, all 4-star ratings and your gone. The thing is, I give 4-star ratings to products I buy on Amazon all the time that I'm perfectly happy with. I save the fifth star for that one product in a dozen that is over-the-top amazing. So why is Uber expecting a driver to earn mostly 5-star ratings? First, it's helpful to understand how Uber manages passenger feedback. Here the Uber uncertainty principle is in effect. An Uber driver gets four pieces of information regarding passenger feedback:

1. A counter indicating how many fares have rated the driver 5 stars (*only* 5 stars)
2. A % average of cumulative star ratings

3. A one word summary of any *negative* comment entered by the fare (but not the actual comment)

4. The complete text of any *positive* comment the fare may have typed in

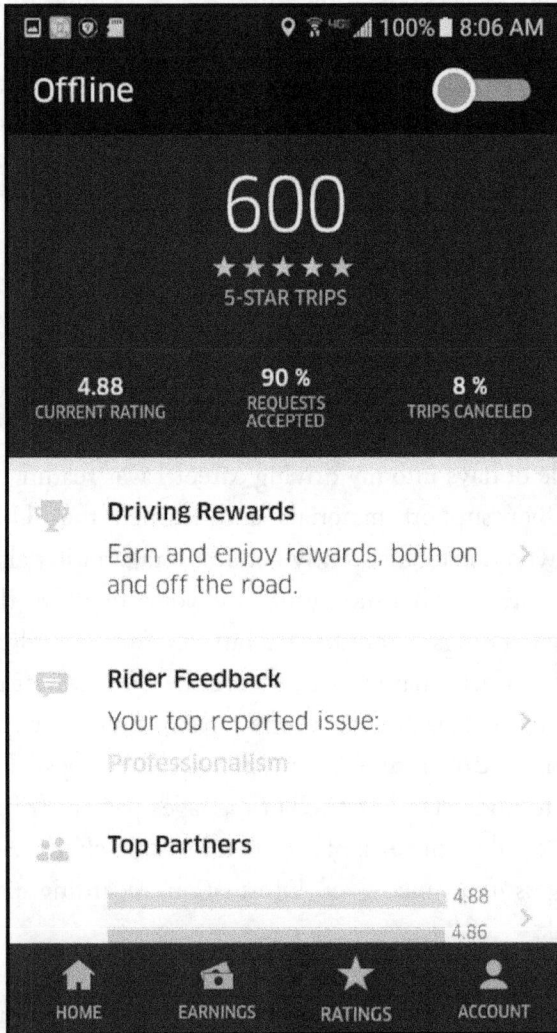

It's hard for a driver to break above 4.9 stars

So what does it all mean? I think what's obviously happening here is that Uber never wants a driver to be able to make the connection between a negative feedback report and the fare who tendered the report. This includes any star rating less than 5. Uber drivers often take passengers home. *The driver knows where the person lives.* To support this architected anonymity Uber even gives the fare an extended period of time to rate the ride (*conversely, the driver must rate the fare immediately in order to get back on the grid and take additional trip requests*). I'm sure the last thing Uber likely feels it needs is a few stories about a driver carrying out retribution on a rider whom they felt submitted an unfair report or star rating.

OK. Fair enough, but unfortunately this system prevents a driver from ever knowing the circumstances of what lead to a low star rating (less than 5) or any other negative feedback. In fact, Uber suppresses any negative comments from being seen by the driver at all... even anonymously... even in delayed fashion. Instead, the driver has a "**Rider Feedback**" button within the driver app which contains a "**Comments**" tab, but only positive comments are noted. There is also an adjacent "**Issues**" screen, but that screen on my app was always empty, even though I occasionally had one word critique summaries appear elsewhere. Out of 1,000+ rides the word "Navigation" appeared twice, as did the word "Professionalism" (again, twice). Yes, in spite of an always empty Issues screen these generically worded critiques, which were titled "Your top reported issue", appeared on occasion. At the end of the day the driver gets minimal guidance as to their mistakes.

Uber states that a driver will be terminated if the average star rating from fares drops to an "unacceptable" level. They further state that the actual threshold varies by region. For Santa Barbara County (where I was driving) the magic number is 4.6.

4. point. 6. Hmm. Every idea I had spawned about having goodies and charge cords, and driving with care and alacrity, and treating passengers with respect no matter who they were, or what they looked like, or what condition they were in... well, Uber had already thought of all that, and the company felt that most passengers will give up a maximum rating if all that happens.

I have to say Uber may be right. I did my best on every ride but inevitably some rides had problems. Yet my score never dipped to 4.6. A few times my navigation to point B was poor. One time I made a fare five minutes late for a wine tasting appointment (mistake in navigation) and I **knew** the gentleman who had ordered the ride would down-rate me. And indeed my score dropped that day. The man had entered the car in a foul mood -ostensibly because his companion was still dillydallying in the hotel room- but he just seemed to be mad at the world. So that was a ride I couldn't afford a mistake on, and when one occurred I paid for it.

On at least a couple of occasions I got nicked for not being professional. This was probably due to shooting my mouth off (you never know for sure). Here is where it gets tricky. I learned early on that where an Uber ride dramatically departs from a taxi ride is in the realm of drive / rider interaction. Almost universally riders want to interact with the driver. Unlike the proto-typical taxi ride where silence is a well-worn option, Uber passengers are often affected by the attitude and demeanor of the driver. I would see this over and over. Riders would tell me stories of a quiet Uber ride with no driver inter-action and how it made them feel uncomfortable (*"The driver*

said nothing!"). So, I would interact with my fares. Most of
them tacitly demanded it. I would make jokes. They would
laugh. But I think at times I may have gone too far. The wrong
joke. An inadvertent comment. Getting too familiar with the
passenger. Who knows?

All in all I've come to believe that no Uber driver should
examine their behavior too closely for the odd critique here and
there. We live in the 'Yelp' age of consumer feedback. Which is
helpful, but as a culture we seem to be getting more willing to
post about any little service related glitch that places a pebble
on our path. Why are we doing that? *Because now we can.* It's a
connected world.

But this is why I say Uber may be right with how they have the
star rating system programmed. Once I got used to the frac-
tional nature of the system, meaning a driver rating of 4.87 is
worlds apart from a 4.67 rating I came to realize that with a
thousand rides under my belt I'd have to have a whole bunch of
4-star (or below) trips to drop the average below 4.6. As it
happened I managed to always keep an average slightly above
what Uber describes as the average for its "top rated drivers."
So I guess I can't complain.

But Uber is not totally off the hook. While the star system as
architected certainly motivated me –the reborn overachiever-
to try *really hard* to get all 5 star ratings, there is still the issue
with how difficult it seems to be to achieve scores in, say, the
4.9+ arena, *even when every ride comes off without a hitch.* The
issue is that Uber does not educate passengers enough about
the star system. People are shocked to learn that a 4-star rating
equates to something having gone wrong. Fares often leave 4
stars even if they had a perfectly acceptable ride. I had a fare
from Denmark tell me they never give Uber drivers 5 stars

because in their home country *"there is no such thing as perfection."*

Note: If you ask ten Uber drivers about star ratings and rider feedback you may well get five different answers. I've seen forum posts where a driver boasted a 4.95 average. Other drivers report that no matter what they do they are always hovering close to the threatened termination threshold. Refer to the Preface.

At the end of the day it is Uber who is in the driver's seat when it comes to setting the rules. The company seems very proactive in making improvements so perhaps in the future more attention will be paid to educating riders as to the importance of the star system. I'm sure most drivers would appreciate not hovering a few fractions away from the threat of having their driving privilege revoked.

Tip Your Uber Driver Please

One question that comes up is should a fare tip their Uber driver. Yes. It is not only typical to tip service personnel in general, the fact is that Uber drivers don't make much money. After gas, insurance, car payments, maintenance costs, and the big one; mileage on the car, there's not all that much left over. Thankfully Uber has finally added a tip option to the rider app. Drivers really appreciate this addition. If you've had a good ride and were delivered safe and sound to your destination your driver will certainly appreciate a little extra. 15-20% seems to be a growing consensus.

Author's note: In mid-2017 Uber commenced its "180 days of change" program to improve the Uber driver's working conditions, and hired a new CEO in August as well. Indeed, welcome changes are have been coming to Uber.

TEN
THEY MOSTLY COME AT NIGHT...
MOSTLY

Uber Stories:

The Almost Carl's Junior Actress

The Man who lost $5,000 in 10 minutes

The Dope Deal

An Impromptu Uber Pool Uncorks a Bottle of Serendipity

Tie a Yellow Light-bar Round the Old Oak Tree

Would you Like to Take a Walk on the Wild Side?

"A day without sunshine is like, you know, night."
- Steve Martin

Aside from driving folks around for wine tasting the bulk of the fares would come in the evening and on through the night. There would be a slight pop around 4 or 5 PM as a few stragglers closed the last of the wine bars in Los Olivos. Then the driver app would start to light up with dinner requests from people wanting to have a few drinks with dinner and not be nagged by the risk of a DUI. Later those same people would be heading back home, or to their hotel, or on to the next watering hole. There were always nighttime pick-ups and drop-offs at the Chumash Casino in Santa Ynez. As the night progressed a good number of the fares were simply about moving intoxicated people from point A to point B. We're talkin' *nice* intoxicated people though. I rarely got a drunk. Another reason why driving in the valley was such a blessing.

If you're at all familiar with ride sharing you've likely heard of its impact on DUI statistics. Drunk driving offenses have gotten so expensive, and ride sharing so dirt cheap, the math has started to weigh in favor of hiring a car whenever the travel plans include drinking followed by driving. Your Uber driver is your DD... your Designated Driver. The service frees up everyone to have a good time and not risk an event that would ruin someone's day. Of course everyone knows this, right? Right. Except I have to tell you that when a Santa Ynez Valley Uber driver pulls into a winery, the parking lot is usually full of wine tasters driving their own cars. It's still a relatively small fraction of tasters that use a ride service.

The police have a high profile presence in the valley. There are few roads and lots of cops. The authorities have also erected electronic highway signs annunciating slogans like **Buzzed Driving is Drunk Driving**. It's all part of a containment strategy that has become more important since the movie Sideways drove herds of wine tasters into the valley. The cops nail the folks who have not yet converted to Uberism. I often told my evening fares that I get "all the smart people". True enough.

Uber Story   🚗   Uber Story   🚗   Uber Story

The Almost Carl's Junior Actress

One night a couple gets in the back seat to go to dinner. The usual conversation takes place about how Uber James came to be driving for Uber. At some point I had started telling my fares that I was writing a book of Uber stories. It was sometime in October when the idea had hit me and it seemed wise to feel people out as to whether a book full of Uber tales was a good idea (virtually every person said yes). This couple in the car tells me that they have loads of interesting stories, if I'd like to hear some. While this offer did not exactly qualify as a bonafide uber story I said yes.

The woman goes. She tells me she does some acting, and asks me if I ever saw the Carl's Junior commercial where the impossibly desirable woman bites into an impossibly desirable thick and juicy burger? Of course I had. The girl told me she had tried out for the commercial. Ha. I had to glance back at her. Yep. She qualified. But she didn't get the part. She's a vegetarian, and after several takes of taking bites out of the burger... she barfed. So much for that commercial.

Uber Story 🚗 Uber Story 🚗 Uber Story

The Man who lost $5,000 in 10 minutes

I get a ride request to pick up a fare at the Chumash Casino. The Prius pulls up to the front entrance. Two men get in the car. One in the back. One in the front. The guy who sits in front is a monster sized man who easily fills the entire seat. We pull out from the casino and on to the 246 heading to downtown Solvang. The first minute of the drive is dead quiet. Then in a mournful voice the man in front says:

Man in front: "James. Ooooh James."

Uber James: "What?"

Man in front: "I just lost five thousand dollars in 10 minutes."

I take measure of his words.

Uber James: "Nah. You're pulling my leg. There's no game in the casino that lets you lose five grand in ten minutes."

Man in front: "Five hundred dollar a hand blackjack.

Uber James: "I believe you."

I did believe him. I hadn't thought of blackjack, but $500 is the maximum bet at many of the casino's blackjack tables. It can be done.

Uber Story   🚗   Uber Story   🚗   Uber Story

The Dope Deal

One night I pick up a crew of locals headed to the Casino. Three guys. But first they need to retrieve one guy's wallet at his apartment. I drive them the opposite way to Buellton to complete the errand. The two guys in the backseat are high on something and when they discover the candy box they attack it and devour its contents.

We arrive at the apartment and the guy in the front seat is picky about where to park the car. He wants to park in a dirt area a ways away from the building. One of the guys from the back seat pops out and jogs around the corner of the building. He's gone for a while. Longer than it takes to grab a wallet.

Suddenly the door opens to the house we are parked in front of. A big dude comes out. The way the layout at this place works we were kind of parked on his turf. Big Dude takes a step or two forward. I see what's coming so I roll down the window and holler "We can move over there if we're trespassing", pointing to in front of the building that we should have been parked at in the first place. He says something to the effect it would be a good idea and walks back inside.

At this point it's clear the mission is *not* to fetch a wallet. It's to score some dope. The two remaining guys get a bit nervous upon sensing I've put 2 + 2 together. "I don't care", I said. That eased their minds.

And I didn't care. There wasn't going to be any trouble, and if there was the car was turned on and pointed in a proper direction for an emergency escape. I didn't worry about much other than being able to operate the vehicle safely on the road. Scoring some pot before an evening of gambling was no concern of mine. As long as no one wanted to use the Uber car for a hit, or as a getaway car, I left people to their own devices.

The missing man finally came out, and we drove to the casino uneventfully.

Uber Story   🚗   Uber Story   🚗   Uber Story

An Impromptu Uber Pool
Uncorks a Bottle of Serendipity

Santa Barbara County does not have UberPOOL, the auxiliary Uber service that allows two different fares to share an Uber car just as fares in New York City might share a taxicab going in the same general direction. None the less, on one occasion I managed to back my way into just such an arrangement. It worked out pretty good though. Early one evening a request comes for a pickup at a Solvang hotel. The fare is two women who have left their husbands back in L.A. to guard the fort while they engaged in a combo business / pleasure excursion to wine country. Tonight it was about dining out and then enjoying some drinks and conversation at a nightclub. I dropped the ladies at Industrial Eats in Buellton for the dinner portion of the evening and continued taking ride requests.

One call in particular comes in from Buellton. I recognized the address. It was a pickup at a boutique winery dubbed 'The Central Coast Group Project'. I had given a couple of rides to its proprietor, Scott Sampler. Scott had provided some juicy wine knowledge on past trips. Did you know for example that some winemakers still crush the grapes by stomping them in bare feet? It's apparently true, and is an effective way to do the crush if the winemaker has made the creative choice to crush with the stems intact. Who knew?

Famous I Love Lucy episode when Lucy stomps grapes in Italy

Tonight it is once again Scott who emerges from the back door of the tiny winery. He is bearing gifts in the form of two loose bottles of wine held by the necks in one hand. I get his door and we are off to a house in a quiet Santa Ynez neighborhood. Presumably Scott was in store for a dinner, and he was apparently not one to go to such an event unarmed.

Now I'm back on the road. A ride or two later and the app lights up for a pickup at Industrial Eats. I recognize the name. It's the two girls I dropped off earlier. I zoom to Eats, load them up, and we go in search of the exact right place for them to extend their evening. By request I drop them at the Landsby hotel, which has a small, comfortable bar called Mad & Vin, which is Danish for Food & Wine.

The girls are worried about being able to find an Uber car later on so I give them my card. "Call me if there's no cars showing on your app and I will come get you when I drop my current fare." It was not unusual for me to give my number out, mostly due to poor cell service in certain areas. My modus operandi was to take such calls, drive to the person's location, then have them request an Uber car. Ride request usually gets routed to the nearest driver.

I pull out of the Landsby and lay in a course for El Rancho Market in Santa Ynez, as my stomach is telegraphing its time for dinner. I'm going to go offline for a while and enjoy some ½ price deli items which always go on sale after 7PM. But not a minute down the road the phone rings. It's the two fun seekers. *"It's dead at the Landsby and we were hoping for a livelier venue."* I explain that I'm going offline to get dinner. They ask if they can tag along while they figure out what to do with their evening. I had been telling them about El Rancho earlier so I said OK and promised them a look. So it's back to the hotel to fetch the girls, and we are now off Uber time.

There was only one problem with this plan. I forgot to actually go **OFFLINE**. Sure enough, as we are approaching Santa Ynez the app lights up. Whoops. It's Scott. He's going to be wanting a ride home from dinner. There's no other Uber drivers online so I compulsively accept the request. We are a matter of blocks from his location and there's really no convenient place to drop the two ladies so we just head over there as is. The outcome of this little impromptu pool is all going to be based upon Scott's acceptance of his car arriving with some unanticipated "luggage". But the girls were cute and friendly, and my finely tuned Jedi senses were informing me that everything was going to be fine.

And it was. I exit the car and walk toward the house to intercept Scott with a story, but before I can figure out what to say he calmly comments, "Oh. A pool." I confirm, give a micro version of the story, and he's fine with that. On the way to his winery he and the ladies spark up a conversation. Suddenly I overhear Scott say "Would you like to taste a little of my wine"?

Now of course in any other context that question could be construed as a line right out of the first book ever written on how to pick up chicks. But that wasn't the case here. The women both had rings on their wedding fingers and Scott was simply being accommodating. There was actually some magic at work because the girls had run out of ideas on where to get a drink and do a little socializing. From their point of view, a boutique winemaker whose products have very restrictive distribution has dropped out of the sky and offers them a tasting. Hello!?

What's more, one of the girls was sort of in the business of promoting wine in her locale down south. So the hint of serendipity that had been decanting for a while was now in bloom. We drove to the winery and they all popped in the back door of the building. I waited in the car, wondering if perchance the chauffer was going to get an invite to the festivities.

The door pops open again. It's Scott.

"James, would you like to come in"?

"Sure!"

The next hour or two was all about hanging out it with the barrels of wine, getting to know Scott's dog and cat; Sergio and Shangy, tasting a variety of Scott's *varietals*, and chatting up a storm. I stuck to water but was feeling quite a part of the whole scene. We learned that before getting into the wine making business Scott had worked as a filmmaker, a writer, and fine artist (if you look at his website at **ccgpwines.com** you will see some of that experience imbedded in the site).

Like the woman from Chapter 9 who found her mojo, and like so many people who find it necessary to perform a mid-course life correction, Scott had found himself pondering what to do after a breakup. In the process of feeling out the next thing... the next thing came along. It happened while Scott was staying with some friends who had a section of undeveloped land on their property. He got the idea to plant some grapevines. Scott Sampler decided to try his hand at wine making.

That was the genesis of The Central Coast Group Project. He now grows his grapes on a plot of land in Los Alamos, processes and stores the wine in Buellton, and has come up with a unique process of making wine that involves "cloned varietals". I could tell you the exact method but then... you know. But, I *can* tell you that the winery's offerings have worked their way onto the wine list of the exclusive L.A. restaurant Spago. That's notable.

So that's what happened on that particular night. The universe brought together all the ingredients for a unique and memorable experience for everyone.

Note: By the way, any Uber executives reading this book, I'm really sorry about that unauthorized pool. It's the only time it even happened and was really quite unintentional.

Behind the camera I was drinking water. Honest!

Uber Story   🚗   Uber Story   🚗   Uber Story

Tie a Yellow Light-bar Round the Old Oak Tree

Again, the thing that's interesting about driving a car for hire is that you never know who might get in your vehicle. On this particular night Uber James got to run with some of the valley's movers and shakers for a while. The driver app lit up with a request from a restaurant mentioned before: Industrial Eats. Eats is on Industrial Avenue in Buellton, and the establishment is testimony as to why Buellton should not be discounted as simply a freeway stop with gas stations and fast food. From where it intersects with Hwy 246, Industrial Avenue at first blush appears as an unassuming industrial parkway. But take a slow drive down the street and several coyly tucked away food and drink gems will make their presence known. Such establishments have gotten a foothold in this commercial district over the past few years. The same thing happened in Santa Barbara a while back when a few square blocks of industrial buildings near the beach were infiltrated by a host of restaurants and beer/wine bars. The area adopted the handle 'The Funk Zone' which is now possibly the number one nighttime Uber destination in Santa Barbara. In Buellton people are starting to refer to the several go-to spots on Industrial Way by the same nickname.

Industrial Eats is a fine example of the farm-to-table mentality that has flooded the valley. Eats initially got its start as a catering business, and later opened a restaurant next door. Tonight my fare, who I had expected to find at the restaurant, appeared in a doorway to the left where the core of the business was headquartered. Hmmm. Interesting. A solo man comes over to the car. "It will be a few minutes. Is that OK?"

Of course it was OK. Anything to do with this place, which had served me a couple of meals I'll never forget, is "OK." If this fare was associated with Eats they could do no wrong in this boy's book.

I did turn the meter on however. Business is business.

Shortly, three gentlemen come out the door. There is a bit of in and out at that door, a bit of meandering around in front, some last minute remarks to unknown persons inside, then the three men then join me in the car. It's turned a bit chilly so I crank up the heat as we pull back on to Industrial Way. The destination is somewhere in Los Olivos, about 10 minutes north via the 101.

The men have had their fill of happy juice and are conversing convivially with each other. They let me in once in a while and slowly I put together a picture of what's going on. One guy is an attorney. The other guy runs a large wine making operation for a billionaire. Not sure about the third man. They are all friends with the owner of Industrial Eats, who had invited them to dinner on this eve. The owner himself did the cooking and had whipped up a number of off-menu delights for his guests. Rather than eat in the main restaurant with the plebeians, the faction had ensconced themselves somewhere in the back area to partake of the feast.

Well excuse me.

Golly gee that sounded like fun. A pack of the valley big dogs getting together for food, drink, and a bit of a confab. Nice work if you can get it.

So now we are in Los Olivos and we drop off the third man. Then it's the businessman's turn to be dropped at his modest but well-tended and gated estate. We're now enroute to the attorney's home when he confides in me: "*That guy we just dropped off? When he is not around and it's a group of us together, we sometimes talk about who the smartest person in the room is. However, when that guy's in the room there is no such debate.*"

Fascinating.

That's all I can tell you without giving up some actual *secret* secrets. But given how much tillable soil there is in the valley how about if we just move along now?

Oh. For you readers who have seen the movie Sideways... at one point we drove by the tree that Thomas Haden Church's character Jack crashes the car into. Now in fact, the tree that Jack supposedly hits in the movie is not actually *the* roadway on a street called Alamo Pintado. As we drove by the tree that night the Prius was a bit toward the right edge of the pavement and we damned near scraped that tree! That's when my new attorney friend filled me in on the history. He thought the tree should somehow be marked given how close it is to the road.

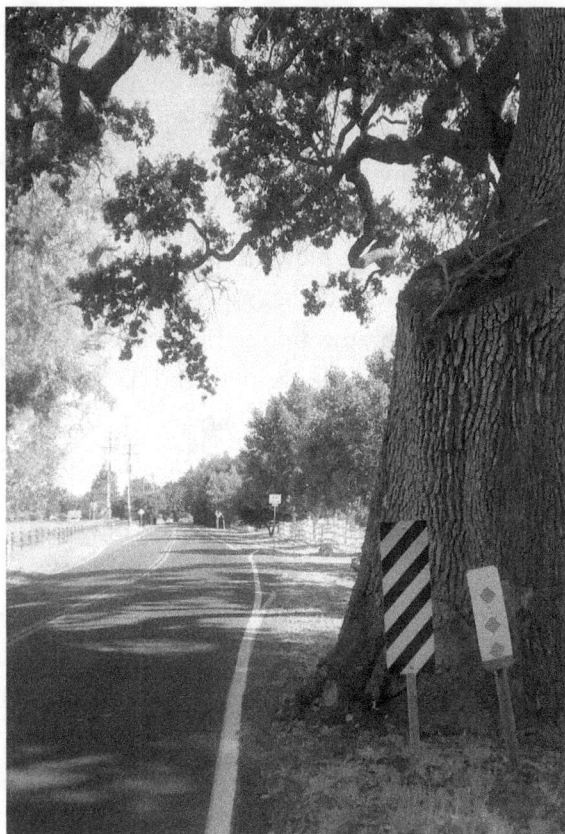

The Tree from the movie Sideways. But not really.

Alamo Pintado by the way is a fun road full of interesting stops like wineries, olive oil tastings, a lavender products store, and my personal favorite stop: a roadside stand where the owner of an organic orchard sells his most delicious apples. So what's not to love?

But as suggested by my passenger they really should install a flashing light to that tree!

Uber Story 🚗 Uber Story 🚗 Uber Story

Would you Like to Take a Walk on the Wild Side?

Actually I'm not sure *which* side of the street the girl I picked up one night worked. But first, in wrapping up this chapter, and given that this *is* sort of a confessions-of-a-taxi-driver type book, I'm assuming you want at least one titillating story. One salacious tale from the back seat to spice up the book. Right? Well this one tale is all I've got. Prepare to be disappointed.

I picked up a young woman at a respectable looking trailer park. This is in Buellton. She wanted to go the casino, which is on the other end of the valley. She gets in and we go. She's on her phone constantly. Not talking. Texting. Suddenly there is a change of plans. We're now going to a motel in Solvang, which is much closer. She's meeting a guy. My finely tuned Jedi senses stir a bit.

So we're driving along and out of the blue the fare offers me something. She offers to do me a *favor*. You know, the thing that guys want more than anything else in the universe?

Whoa. Danger Will Robinson. This was like something out of a pulp novel. My brain makes a dozen calculations, but without pause I reply *"Oh, that's ok."* You see, being well past prime I couldn't figure out what formula was in play to incite such an invitation. Something was not right, and even though there wasn't enough evidence to determine what that something was, I none-the-less decided not to play.

We have a bit of a conversation on the topic where I tell her I'm basically staring down the business end of a bottle of Viagra, and she is assuring me that would not be an issue. My statement, which may or may not have been true, was designed to politely and without incident deflate the matter. The ploy didn't work, but one or two polite declines later and she let it go.

Was she a *she*? Might *that* account for the proposal? Her voice was a bit neutral. Hard to say for sure. It was dark in the back-seat and I hadn't gotten a clear look at my passenger when she got in. I certainly was not interested in playing a round of *The Crying Game*. The matter was fully put to rest though when we arrived at the hotel. She thanked me for the ride and went to meet her date.

I went on with my life, sans regrets.

ELEVEN
UBER JAMES DISCOVERS GOLD IN THE SANTA YNEZ VALLEY

Driving Uber

T-Bone Over Easy

The Van Man

The Girl With the Hair Trigger Finger

Philosophy Corner

"You was definitely in the right.
That geezer was cruisin' for a bruisin'!"
- Anonymous female voice on the track 'Money',
Pink Floyd: Dark Side of the Moon

Driving Uber

It won't surprise you to hear an Uber driver claim that one of the biggest aspects of driving an Uber car is.... driving. The act of driving in traffic. It's the DNA of the job. During the exodus I was driving in the morning, the afternoon, and evening. Never to the point of exhaustion. There were always breaks between rides for meals, naptimes, and gaps in ride requests. But the Prius Super-duper Uber car was often the first to appear on the Uber rider app in the morning, and the last to disappear off the radar at night.

So I was on the streets a lot and this *is* California... full of California drivers. When a ride request came in I would try and get to point A as soon as possible. Safely... legally... but usually pushing toward the outer edge of the envelope. I would often do 10-15 over the speed limit. This was effectively "legal" in so far as a good percent of the traffic was doing likewise and no one was getting ticketed. And it felt safe because my BRAND NEW CAR was in perfect mechanical condition.

Still, by pushing toward the high-side when negotiating traffic, driving at times was reminiscent of slot car racing, or playing a video game. There was a fair amount of maneuvering taking place to overcome the slower drivers, and that tends to diminish the safety buffer.

There is however this notion called conscious, aware driving...

just as there is a thing called careless and lackadaisical driving.
I have always *tried* for the former. One of my *prime directives*
for driving is to never do something that requires another driver
to take evasive action. When you enter traffic the guy behind
you should not have to hit his brakes to avoid hitting you. An
enhanced version of this philosophy is that the guy behind you
should not even have to *think* about hitting his brakes. While
many drivers adopt one version or another of this policy, in
California, the further south you go the more likely the careless
and lackadaisical motif is in vogue.

I grew up in the Bay Area of Northern California and the first
time I drove in Southern California it was astoundingly clear
that the rules were different. It was not at all rare for someone
to ~~pull in front of you~~ cut you off, requiring instant braking to
avoid a collision. This is just business as usual in some southern
locales (and of course in other places in the states and around
the world). I later moved from the Bay Area to Santa Barbara -
which sort of demarcates central and southern California- only
to discover that a great deal of L.A. driving habits had leaked
that far north.

And as it turns out there are a great many SoCal transplants
living in the Santa Ynez Valley, and some seem to have brought
their driving habits with them. There is in fact a broad mix of
drivers in the valley. I was mentioning the challenges of driving
to one of my regular fares, a bartender who sometimes gets
Uber rides after work if his wife has the family car. The man
not only serves drinks but he dispenses tidbits of philosophy
and is a keen observer of the human condition. He broke down
the various categories of valley drivers. Along with the local
residents, there's the foreign tourists (be afraid, be very afraid),
the wine drinkers, the occasional drunk, and last but not least
the 'entitled LA drivers' running around in Cadillac Escalades

and Eddie Bauer Ford Explorers, just to name a couple of models typical of that ilk- some of whom should be sporting the old bumper sticker that reads "**Yes, as a matter of fact I do own the whole damned road**".

T-Bone Over Easy

All of the above is a backdrop for imparting a few driving stories and how Uber James was fortunate enough to be able to convert some lemons into to a nice glass of lemonade. It was a realization I'm quite grateful for.

First, I was driving back from Lompoc one afternoon in September and was approaching Buellton. This is Hwy 246. The speed limit changes incrementally from 65MPH down to 45MPH as you approach the city limits. Some people notice, some don't. Well into the 45MPH zone I suddenly spot an accident. It is a rollover accident at a 4-way intersection involving a pickup truck with a camper shell and a sedan. The sedan is badly smashed at the front and right side, and had been pushed by the collision to the curb of one corner of the intersection. The pickup truck is upside down in the exact center of the intersection. The scene was at the same time both comical and tragic. By all appearances the pickup had T-boned the sedan when the sedan pulled into what is an uncontrolled intersection.

The accident had occurred within the last minute or two. A couple of cars had pulled over and were preparing to render aid. As I roll through the intersection there is a clear view of the occupants inside the truck. It is two people. They are conscious, looking straight ahead, and calmly sitting in their seats exactly as they would have been while driving down the highway moments ago. Except they were upside down!

The site was surreal. Clearly the passengers were belted in. Given that I was in the middle of picking up a fare and that others were responding I decided to call in the accident and continue on. Only days later was any info available as to injuries/fatalities. I made the inquiry to a cop who had been on the scene. No one had been hurt. The cop followed up his answer with the remark *"Seatbelts save lives"*.

The accident left a permanent mark on *me* though. I couldn't stop thinking about it. I've driven by plenty of accidents but had never seen one so up-close and personal. To see those people trapped inside their vehicle and just dangling. The image put the hook in me. I made a decision to stop rushing to every Uber pickup. In fact I made an agreement with myself to never again drive more than 5MPH over the speed limit. This has not been an easy promise to keep. There are times, like on a single lane highway where all the cars are going 10 or more over, that doing the speed limit actually reduces safety. And sometimes I just forget and bad habits resurface. But for the most part I've been able to make a practice of never going more than 5 over. It feels great.

The Van Man

But the rollover accident is not the story this chapter was titled from. There's more. I had a couple of confrontations with other drivers. And the count may have gone up if something hadn't changed. My Uber passengers may have been riding around in a judgment-free zone, but I sure as hell was judging other drivers on the roadway.

In one instance I was driving through downtown Buellton on the 246. That's the main drag through town. The street is laid out with two lanes in either direction, and in lieu of a center divider there is one of those shared turn lanes that allow vehicles from either direction to safely initiate left turns, as well as to act as a buffer for vehicles merging into traffic from the other side of the street.

So I'm driving westbound in the lane just adjacent to the turn lane. Traffic is moving at speed. A camper van pulls onto the highway from the left, crosses the two lanes of opposing traffic and navigates into the buffer lane, just ahead of my car, which is in the traffic lane. All is well.

However, instead of getting up to speed before merging into the traffic lane, the van simply continues without pause across the buffer lane and right into the traffic lane, dead in front of my car. I had no choice but to hit the brakes.

I am steamed at the driver's cavalier behavior and wishing there was a way to give that so-and-so a piece of my mind. These kinds of situations were happening frequently and were starting to get to me. I had nothing to do at the moment... *so I decided to follow the van.* Yeah. I'm going to follow the vehicle until there's an opportunity to deliver a scolding. The van continues on the 246 for about a mile, the Prius conspicuously trailing behind. The vehicle finally pulls left into a trailer park of some kind. It looked like home for whoever is behind the wheel. I follow the culprit into the Lion's den.

I had no idea who was driving. Man. Woman. Little person. Big person. Regardless, I wasn't going to let the situation escalate. The flash of anger had worn off and I was mostly interested in letting the person know that their actions have consequences. The van continues to the interior of the park. I get a view of a male in the driver's seat as the vehicle rounds a corner. A car exiting the park approaches the van from the other direction and both vehicles stop opposite each other. The occupants have a confab. The van then continues forward about twenty yards and turns left into a parking space. The other car is frozen on the road. I ease forward and reach the stationary vehicle. It's occupied by two elderly people. I say to them *"Is that guy a friend of yours?"* They respond in the affirmative. *"Well he may be drinking and driving. I nearly crashed into him in town."*

I of course had no clue as to whether the man had been drinking or not, but such a suggestion usually brings people to attention, as folks are more conditioned to detest drunk drivers as opposed to downright careless and dangerous drivers. The couple in the car are quite composed and inform me that the man is elderly and has glaucoma. Ah ha. That might explain things. I tell the couple that I'm going to talk to the gentleman. They acquiesce but their car stays riveted in the lane.

Meanwhile the Van Man exits his vehicle and starts walking away, cutting across the lane where it makes a sharp left turn past the parking area. I pull the Prius forward and around the corner. In the meantime *another* car is exiting the park, and the Van Man, on foot and in the middle of crossing the lane, intercepts that vehicle too.

My presence is having the intended effect. The man is paying attention. And he's worried. He engages in conversation with the driver of the new car for a few seconds before I catch up alongside him, still in my car. The guy he's taking to is a huge biker type. I ignore that intimidating variable for the moment and go to work on the Van Man. *"You're dangerous! Your friends just ratted you out. If your eyesight is impaired then maybe you should think about not driving any longer. It happens to all us all eventually. If I hadn't been paying close attention I would have hit you."*

The man reacts in a superficially non-pulsed fashion, but I can see he's agitated. "*I know you saw me!*" he exclaims.

Wait a minute. *I know you saw me?* That seemed to be a 'tell' that poor vision was not the offender here. For him to know I saw him, means *he* must have seen *me*. So the guy apparently had pulled a standard issue yeah-I'm-rudely-cutting-you-off-but-I- know-you-won't-hit-me" move.

I ignore the reveal for a moment.

Van Man, never leveraging the glaucoma excuse, now threatens to call the Sheriff. I counter with "*Go ahead. I am considering calling the CHP and having them administer a breathalyzer test.*" The reply was a gambit but I'm thinking it might keep the big dude in the other car at bay. It does. He remains seated, eyes on the action but wordless. Van Man refutes my accusation but does not dial 9 1 1. We fence with words for a minute or two, then I realize my hand is just about played out. I had served up a thin slice of revenge hot and fresh from the oven by embarrassing Mr. Van Man in front of his friends. It was now time to retreat. What had stood out in the conversation with Van Man was that he had a ready answer for every accusation I threw at him. His answers were almost practiced, like he'd been there before. My last remark was to assert "*You have an answer for everything... and that's your problem!*" He sort of folded on that one. His face fell a bit and he went silent. The remark had found a soft spot. I put the car in reverse and backed out of the park.

The Girl With the Hair Trigger Finger

With the prior incident now in the history books I continue my day, giving the odd ride here and there. Suddenly another close encounter occurs.

I'm returning home after a fare. About a block from the motel a female motorist runs a stop sign. Her car plunges into a T intersection a few yards in front of the Prius. I'm able to stop in time, and reflexively throw my hands up in a *"What the hell are you doing?"* motion. The 20-something woman driver, now stopped, replies with the middle finger of her left hand in a *"F you for even asking"* motion, then zooms by me.

Ignoring the provocation I pull forward to the motel, park the car, and get out to enter my room. Glancing down the street I see the car that ran the stop sign parking in front of an apartment building. The woman lives three blocks from me! I couldn't resist the urge to go ask her why she flipped me off. It was just too tempting a target. So, back in the car and down the street we go.

Again, I wanted to make a point, but was not going to let the situation escalate. I wasn't mad. I just wanted to see how the woman would behave when confronted by the person she had just disrespected with both her car and her finger. Would there be an apology... or more finger pointing?

This situation required a totally different approach as it was a woman this time. She and a girlfriend are still sitting in her car as I pull up alongside. I smile and beckon the girl to roll down her window. She scowls and refuses. What happened next is funny. If it had been filmed the video no doubt would have gone viral on YouTube.

The girl and I somehow manage to carry on a coherent, understandable conversion in sign language with the window up. I mouth words and sign, *"Why did you flip me off?."* She snarls a reply in the same format, *"Because you threw up your hands in astonishment"*, as she mimics my response at the stop sign. Clearly the young lady was not tolerating any criticism of her act. Then she asks me to leave, with a motion like a woman would shoo away a pesky man at a bar. I decline. This goes on a bit until she asks if I would prefer her to call the police as she makes the universal sign of someone talking on the phone. I smile and nod my head yes.

Now that was definitely a bluff on my part. The thought of the police coming struck fear in my heart. First, because I was the one who pulled my car up to her's. I could easily be perceived as the aggressor regardless of whether she ran a stop sign or had run over my dog for that matter. Second, she is a young female and I am a middle aged man. Stop sign or no stop sign I wasn't likely to come out of a 3-way with the police unscathed.

The girl had checkmated me but fortunately she didn't know it. She didn't call 911. We argued for another moment, then I put the car in gear and shouted out "Be nice... Be nice to people... Be nice to people!", while all the time she's making an ugly face and shaking her head no. The Prius and I then retreated back to the motel.

> *"Be kind, for everyone is in a great battle"*
> *-anonymous Roman soldier'*

Philosophy Corner

So let's pull back to the big picture regarding how we humans deal with the irritations of life. We all have a different set of triggers that gets our goat. Some people have more triggers. Some fewer. Fair enough? Do you know anyone who has no triggers? People that aren't bothered by anything at all are a rare breed. Some spiritual disciplines encourage students to let go of their *attachments*. Once you do that nothing is capable of bugging you. But if you've ever tried to let go of your attachments you may have found it's not so easy. I've tried. It's not easy.

However, there may be what could be termed an interim solution to our peeves. It's a technique that may be easier to achieve than detachment. Let me explain. About 20 years ago I was feeling the need for a little religion. I had abandoned Catholicism at age 18 but was now prompted to seek a philosophy of how to live in a way that prepares one for what may come subsequent to this mortal life. I picked up a copy of Houston Smith's 'The World's Religions'. The book lists and describes all the major religions of the world, which run from Buddhism to Taoism. As it happened, none of the faiths fully resonated.

However, there was one significant take away from Smith's book. What jumped out was a common thread running through the varied disciplines and belief structures. *It was simply a notion of putting other people first. To put others ahead of yourself.*

Put others ahead of yourself. Put. Others. Ahead. Of. Yourself.

Hmm. Not an unfamiliar notion. It's a concept many are likely familiar with. It's another way to say don't be self-ish. So what's the big deal? The big deal, if there is either temporal *or* spiritual value to the idea, is that it's a philosophy that needs to be remembered... validated.... reinforced, and unfortunately we don't live in a society that does so. If anything, it's quite the opposite. From the post-World War II Baby boomer generation, code named the "Me" generation, right down to the social-media attentive Millennials, who could be code named the "Selfie" generation, the notion of putting others first is not exactly baked into the cake of modern western culture. And since the whole world seems to be getting more and more westernized it may be fair to say that those who truly put the needs of their fellow human beings ahead of their own needs are in the minority.

But for whatever reason that tidbit scavenged from Smith's book resonated. Back then I had made an attempt to adopt the principle into daily life. It seemed to work. It doesn't kill you to put others first. In fact quite often it benefits both parties. I'm not claiming an instant karma effect that pays the do-gooder immediate dividends. But in my experience when you have those moments of actually allowing others to go ahead of you, many of life's problems evaporate.

The notion of putting others first can manifest simply as letting that person with only three items in their shopping cart take cuts at the checkout stand. On the end of the spectrum we hear stories of people putting their life at risk in say, a plane crash, helping others exit the plane ahead of them. *We hold such people up because they are heroically betraying the reflexive impulse of self-preservation when taking such action.*

The only problem with the put-others-first philosophy is that even if you are willing, you have to *remember* to use the technique! You have to be mindful of the act of putting others first, because there's that voice in your head constantly arguing the other way.

So I would go for long periods of time completely forgetting the philosophy.

Grapes to Wine... Lemons to Lemonade

When I first started driving Uber I was not being mindful of the putting-others-first principle. Not with regards to other motorists anyway. With traffic wearing on my nerves more and more, and given that it was my "job" to drive in traffic, this was a problem. Something needed to be done before it became a *big* problem. I racked my brains for a solution. It was then that the put-others-first method came to mind. I knew the technique would work because I had employed it before with positive results. I had been unconsciously employing the technique with Uber passengers. And now, reminded again of the philosophy, I began using it in traffic.

And everything changed.

I went back in my mind and let go of any encounter that was still soaking up brain cycles by choosing to let those drivers have their way. To say OK, you made a mistake, you were distracted, you succumbed to selfishness. Whatever. It's OK. **I choose to have let you go first**. Even if you ran a stop sign!

From that day forward navigating traffic in the valley became less and less of an issue. The energy of all the typical traffic shenanigans was unwinding. As long as I remembered in the moment, or even later, to *choose* to let that car that was forcing its way through traffic... to go right ahead, the resentment did not build up. Somehow giving permission in my own mind prevented any bad feelings from taking root

Selflessness is the Longer View

I suppose achieving a full state of detachment accomplishes the same effect. In my view though –and I stress that this is one person's view- we perhaps have more immediate control over making a conscious choice to put-others-first. It can be **nearly impossible** at times to make that choice, but it is a *choice*. Achieving detachment is a noble goal that I'm open to. However, when I can remember to simply engage the idea of taking attention off my "self", situations often resolve themselves.

But again, selfishness tends to dominate human affairs. If we look to where global power is concentrated -arguably in the mega corporations- which use profits to beget more profits by distorting the system of regulations designed to prevent a mere few from bettering themselves at the expense of the planet's inhabitants, it can be argued that we're all living under an umbrella of selfishness. We see constant examples of selfishness apparently paying off. This top-down mentality tends to erode personal efforts to achieve selflessness as fear and an every-man-for-himself survival instinct tugs at our psyches.

So one must be introspective as to whether one is going to surrender to that every-man-for-himself impulse, which on the surface may appear to be *the way* to survive... or one must find a reason to break with the pack and choose to live a more compassionate life... if that resonates inside. We have little control over other people's behavior so all we can do is exert what control we have over our own behavior. And there is an argument that living a life based on such principles is of benefit to both the individual (the self) as well as all mankind, *due to the notion that a rising tide floats all boats.*

"temet nosce" (*know thyself*)
- *Inscription on a plaque in the Oracles' kitchen: 'The Matrix'*

In my experience the putting-others-first principle is not a blindly followed discipline. There is a degree of discrimination involved. To use an extreme example, if a man is driving his pregnant wife who's in labor to the emergency room he doesn't let all the cars trying to get in the left turn lane to the hospital take cuts. It seems contradictory but we have to take care of *ourselves* first, to be in a position to put others first. It's not always easy to discern the difference. I often don't hesitate to think of my own needs in certain circumstances. Conversely, I've been in many situations where on the surface it appeared I'd be greatly disadvantaged by letting the other person go ahead of me, yet did so anyway, only to later learn that both of us benefitted from the act. Discerning the difference may take practice. It's very personal. Everyone has their own threshold. But just being aware of the option helps make one mindful that there is a choice at hand as we go through our day.

The Broader Landscape

One thing that guides me in making the choice to apply the put-others-first principle is another element from my "failed" investigation into religion. It slightly expands on the core principle we've been discussing. In trying to answer the question posed earlier -*how to live in a way that prepares one for what may come subsequent to this mortal life*- there again seems to be some degree of consensus among various spiritual disciplines that focuses on the treatment of our fellow human beings. It again involves the idea of not always obeying our primal survival instinct and to instead treat others well, to never take advantage, to never use others as a means to further your own personal goals... and to have mercy, compassion, and tolerance toward others when they fail to treat you in a like manner. This is a more encompassing philosophy that includes the putting-others-first element. The promise of such a moral code, some say, is a rich afterlife.

But wait. With that last paragraph, certainly that last sentence, we are now immersed into what at first glance could be construed to be a *theory* supported by supposition, extrapolation, and possibly unprovable notions. For whatever benefit the philosophy of compassion toward others may return in the here and now, how can one know for certain of any further returns down the line?

In my own view, one can't. At least I don't think there is any way to *know*.

At this juncture the word "faith" normally enters the discussion. Faith is great, and there is no argument being made here against faith, but in my personal view, for whatever it's worth, just as there may be an alternative to detachment when it comes to tolerating the behavior of our fellow humans, so too there may be a way to adopt the larger notion of compassionate treatment of others even if blind faith happens to fall short.

What I came to realize is this: If I chose to blindly adopt the philosophy of compassion in whole ... and upon passing from this mortal coil were to discover that I'd been dead wrong, that there was no penalty for living a selfish life, *I could accept that.* I can live my life NOW knowing I may have chosen the wrong path.

At the same time I realized that if I lived a life of selfishness and bending others to serve my own self-centered goals, and upon passing learned that I was dead wrong, *I could NOT live with that.*

In fact I would even go so far as to say that even if it turns out there is no afterlife, I still have no regrets. Meaning, I feel comfortable living my day-to-day life NOW with the philosophy of compassion as a goal no matter what may come later.

So at the end of the day it was an easy choice. Faith need not play a part. Again, not that there's anything wrong with faith. It's just that for me, as with being unable to hold onto the state of detachment that comes and goes, I never have to worry about "losing faith".

And that foundation may be what gave me the strength to employ the put-others-first principle in traffic when my "instincts" often strongly advised otherwise.

By the way, I fail often. I think I need a plaque above the door to my house that reads P-O-F. Regardless, all one can do is to apply the philosophy as one can. The immediate reward is the lightness and freedom you experience at times when letting go of your judgment against people for having trespassed on you. It's a self-affirming, win-win philosophy.

TWELVE
LOVE AND MARRIAGE IN THE SANTA YNEZ VALLEY

Uber Stories:

The Conspiracy

The Fabulous Bachelorette Party Girls (Group A)

The Fabulous Bachelorette Party Girls (Group B)

Bachelorette Party Girls A Redux

Uber James Inadvertently Creeps Out the A Team

Uber James Gets Stood Up at the Altar - Occurrence A

Uber James Gets Stood Up at the Altar - Occurrence B

Let's Makes a Habit of it

It Was Mine to Lose... And I Nearly Did

"I love being married. It's so great to find that one special person you want to annoy for the rest of your life."
-Rita Rudner

Besides drawing in wine tasters, tourists, gamblers, foodies, horse lovers, and others... the Santa Ynez Valley is a magnet for weddings. Hundreds of weddings take place in the valley each year. The Uber traffic would often start on Thursday with the early birds flocking in to explore and romp prior to the main event. On Friday evenings all the Uber driver apps in the valley would light up as wedding attendees made their way to and from rehearsal dinners. Saturday would see a burst of requests to shuttle folks to and from the weddings. And Sunday mornings would often bring an early morning blip in requests from people who had wisely let a friend take them home the night before and now needed to retrieve their car. Later in the weekend requests would come in for runs to the airport.

So there are certainly some wedding stories to tell. First though we're going set the controls of the Wayback machine to an earlier point in the mating game and be a fly on the wall to see how one man set the table for popping the question.

Uber Story 🚗 Uber Story 🚗 Uber Story

The Conspiracy

I got a request for a pickup somewhere north of Santa Ynez. It was a tiny café in the middle of nowhere. As I pulled into the parking area two young women ran over to the car and hopped in.

Woman #1: "We're so happy to see you!"

Woman #2: "You saved us!"

Uber James (pulling onto the road): "Great. What's up?

The story was that the ladies had surreptitiously come to the café to set up a table for two friends due to arrive shortly. The two friends were a man and a woman. The man and the woman were boyfriend and girlfriend. *Boyfriend* was going to propose to *Girlfriend* at lunch, and Girlfriend had no clue what was coming. So obviously she didn't know her two friends were at the café prepping for the event.

The whole event had been architected. What was by all appearances in Girlfriend's eyes a family weekend getaway that she just happened to bring Boyfriend along to, was in fact an engagement party that scads of family and friends had been invited to and were all sequestered away until post-question popping festivities were due to commence.

So what had gone wrong that required an Uber car? The vehicle that the two girls had come in wouldn't start. They were stranded and had to get out of the area PDQ before Boyfriend and Girlfriend arrived. That's why the girls were so relieved to see the car they had summoned appear.

I had only one question. You can imagine what it was...

Uber James: "How do you know she's gonna say yes?"

In unison: "She's gonna say yes."

OK. That could only mean that Girlfriend had been confiding in others that she was in love with Boyfriend and wanted to marry him. It was just a question of when Boyfriend was going to get off the dime... and that time had now come.

So how did it all turn out? I have no idea. Never saw any of the group again. Such is the life of an Uber driver. All we can do at this juncture is celebrate what a blessing ride sharing is with a silly little jingle:

Ode to the Uber Car

Uber car
Uber car
Gliding through the air
Uber car
Uber car
Uber everywhere
Feared by the cabs
Loved by the hoods
Uber car
Uber car

Uber Story 🚗 Uber Story 🚗 Uber Story

The Fabulous Bachelorette Party Girls (Group A)

In between the proposal and the marriage comes the ritual of the bachelor/bachelorette party. These happen in the valley too. There is one weekend in particular I won't soon forget. Midday on a Saturday an Uber request came in from a secluded neighborhood north of Solvang. It's a road rarely traveled by tourist cars. But Uber cars.... yeah. I find the address.

The house is at the end of a long steep winding driveway. A few cars are parked in front of a beautiful ranch style house. The Prius joins the other cars. This is what I love about Uber. I had no idea who was going to come out of the house. As it happened, four lovely 20-something women emerge. They are dressed for an outing. The girls pile in the car and buckle up. I learn they are on a bachelorette party weekend and that they've rented the house on Airbnb.

A bachelorette *weekend*? Times have changed. Back when I was thinking in terms of such events bachelor/ette parties lasted an evening. Rarely even an overnighter. The most exciting thing that ever happened on my watch was one time when the bachelorette party crashed the bachelor party. But that is a story for another time. The four girls in *this* story inform me that bachelorette weekends are a matter of course now, and it's not unusual to sweep the bride-to-be away to a far-off location. The very presence of these bonnie lasses was proof. They had driven the several hundred miles up from SoCal to show their engaged friend a good time before her life changed in inexorable and everlasting ways.

The first stop on the good-time tour is a winery. For reference purposes we will refer to the girls as Bachelorette #1, Bachelorette #2, Bachelorette #3, and Bachelorette #4. The girls and I hit it off quite well. I seem to come off harmless and trustworthy to women these days, which I suppose is a sign of my advanced age. There was a time when I would have been disconcerted by the labels *harmless* and *trustworthy*, but in this context such attributes were a blessing.

As we make the rounds I'm included in much of the conversation, and of course the girls get the whole evacuated-from-home tale. They were fascinated. They LOVE Big Sur. It's all wonderfulness in the car and I'm enjoying having these smiling beauties all to myself. Nice work if you can get it.

The music is set to post-tasting playlist level III. One of the ladies shouts out "James, you're a rock star." What a nice compliment. I retort "Thank you. That's the nicest thing anyone has said to me in a long time." I'm mentioning this because of something that will happen later. Then it's getting later and the girls head back to their secret fortress and cut me loose. It would not be the last I would see of the group.

Uber Story 🚗 Uber Story 🚗 Uber Story

The Fabulous Bachelorette Party Girls (Group B)

Once back **ONLINE** I picked up a couple of short uneventful rides. Then the app lit up for a pickup in a remote location. It was another Airbnb rental. I arrive, the door to the house opens, and out streams... four lovely 20-something ladies. They were up from SoCal on a bachelorette weekend. Weird. I couldn't help wondering if I'd fallen into one of those parallel universes again. Or gone down some kind of rabbit hole where everything looks the same, only different? While I ponder the possibility of a rip in the space/time continuum, the girls, who have already gotten a head start on their tasting experience slink into the backseat, with the overflow girl touching down on the seat next to me. Then we're off.

I switch mental ponderings for a moment to reflect on the possibility this set of bachelorette ladies would like to meet the other set of bachelorette ladies. A different voice in my head immediately replies "No you idiot. Different worlds!" Well OK now.

It's another great ride. A warm rapport develops as the passengers traverse the wineries. At some point the girls are done and want to go home. There is a passing utterance about inviting Uber James in for Pizza, but the motion isn't seconded. This was fine. I would have been unable to decline such a gracious invitation, and it seemed best to quit while I was ahead. I dropped the tipsy foursome at their weekend rental and got a nice hug from each girl. Life is good.

Uber Story   🚗   Uber Story   🚗   Uber Story

Bachelorette Party Girls A Redux

The following morning there is a summons on the driver app to pick up the *first* set of bachelorette girls. They are off to breakfast, or maybe it was brunch, so I'm not sure why they needed an Uber car. Maybe they were planning to imbibe a Ramous Fizz or perhaps a glass of champagne with the meal.

I whisk the food seekers off to the breakfast place. When the girls pile out of the car bachelorette #1 in the front seat pulls something from her purse and hands it to me. The other girls glance back as they head to the building. It's a Rock Star button! A round lapel button with the phrase "Rock Star" on it. I ask them how the hell they came up with that, but there are no replies. They're off to breakfast.

Proudly, I affix the button to the dash.

That rock star button sits on the dash to this day

The girls must have caught a different Uber car home because I did not see them for a while. I picked up various fares throughout the day. There was a fare in the car when all of a sudden we hear a strange sound. It was inside the car. Priuses make a lot of weird noises but this was a new one. The passengers looked puzzled. We would hear the sound intermittently. On. Off. On. Off. This goes on for like ten minutes. We couldn't figure out exactly where the noise was coming from.

Suddenly my phone rings. It's Bachelorette #1 from the A team. She left her phone in my car. Her phone? We search the car and the phone is found lodged between the front passenger seat and the center console. Mystery solved. People have such varied ring tones! I promise to bring the phone by as soon as I drop the current fare. That happens, I go offline and head over to the A team's headquarters. This was going to be interesting. Why? Because it was sort of an impromptu visit. I mean at least one person knew I was coming but it wasn't like the crew was getting ready for a road trip. It was an opportunity to see this species in its native habitat. What were these bachelorette beauties going to be up to? Had they received a parachute drop of male strippers or something?

I pull in the driveway. Voices are coming from outside. I glance to the left, past a veranda, to an open grassy area with a few scattered trees. There are the girls. They are... *sitting on the lawn quietly talking amongst themselves.*

That completed that bit of research. These were good girls. Makes me wish I was young again.

Uber Story   🚗   Uber Story   🚗   Uber Story

Uber James Inadvertently Creeps Out the A Team

As luck would have it I got bachelorette Part A once more that weekend. They were going out to dinner at the one of the best restaurants in the Santa Ynez Valley; SY Kitchen. Guess what the "SY" stands for? I dropped them off and assured them that I would stay on duty to be sure they had a ride home. Acknowledging the offer they went into the eatery... and did not emerge for a long time.

I was giving rides to people as each fare rang in on the driver app. After a few hours fatigue was starting to set in. It was time to think about shutting down operations for the night. But the question was, had the A team already found a ride home? They had been in the restaurant for two or three hours. They *must* have gone home by now. But I didn't want to retire until sure. I drove to the restaurant and pondered the best way to determine if they were still inside. I really didn't want to simply walk inside and look around. It seemed a little obvious. Like I was checking up on them. Right? So instead I thought I would be a clever lad and take a walk along the outside of the building where a nice big picture window lends a view to the main seating area. I could surreptitiously glance in and see if the girls were in there.

The only problem with my plan was that as I passed in front of the window the girls were seated at a table *right next to the window*. They all looked up simultaneously and saw Uber James peering in. They didn't smile. In a single moment of wrong planning I had done the thing that any self-respecting middle aged man dreads doing; creeping out a bunch of young women. Not good.

I tried to climb out of the hole I was waist deep in. All the girls were now looking down at their plates except bachelorette # 4. I made eye contact with #4, attempted to turn the corners of my startled mouth up, and made a sign by touching my index and middle finger to my left eye and then pointing the fingers at her. I then pointed to the car and made an exit. Hopefully #4 translated my sign language as "I was just checking to see if you were here. I will be waiting in the car."

And that's where Uber James waited. After a bit the driver app started flashing. It was a pickup at the SY Kitchen. In a moment the A team popped out and headed toward the Prius. Smiling, the girls showed no leftovers from the earlier incident as they approached the car. Like I said, these were pretty classy gals. They buckled in and off we went to the house. Something *had* to be said so I tried to explain what had happened. They listened politely and even laughed a little. Bachelorette #3 said to me "To be honest James when I saw you at the window I was both a little creeped out and a little comforted at the same time."

Her comment made perfect sense and seemed to clear the air. In short order the group was dropped safely at bachelorette central and we all went on with our lives. The button on my dashboard is still there however.

"I can't hear your words.
Your actions are speaking too loudly."
-adapted from a Ralph Waldo Emerson quotation

A constant reminder while driving Uber was how often people say they are going to do something... then not do it. This is a pervasive and generational phenomenon, at least in American culture. If you think about how many people you know who always do exactly what they say, is it not a rather short list? How seriously do we take statements such as "I'll call you next week." "I'll stop by tomorrow." "I'll let you know when the job opens up." "I'll pay you on Tuesday for a hamburger today."

For the most part such behavior is accepted. People do it to us. We do it to others. And we usually don't get called on it when our words turn into vapor rather than action. It's sort of an unwritten rule, because if you *do* call someone out for not keeping their word you may get an apology... or just as likely an offended someone. The following is an example of this phenomenon manifesting itself in the world of ride sharing:

Uber Story   🚗   Uber Story   🚗   Uber Story

Uber James Gets Stood Up at the Altar - Occurrence A

I pick up a man and a woman in Santa Ynez. They are off on a couple's day to taste some wine. A conversion ensues. They tell me they are getting married that weekend in the valley. A hundred people will attend. They ask if there's anything I can do to round up some Uber cars for the event. The couple claims that most of the guests will be leaving their cars at their hotel and will need a ride home after the reception.

I say "OK. I can get in touch with some other drivers and let them know." The couple is delighted to hear this. They underscore that the wedding and reception will be held at Roblar Winery, which has a hard ending time of 10PM for events.

I knew Roblar. It's just off Hwy 154, roughly halfway between Santa Ynez and Los Olivos. Roblar is a popular stop for wine tasters. On an Uber ride the month before a couple reported that not only is the wine and ambience great, they were allowed to venture out among the vines to taste the grapes.

I had also delivered the son of the Roblar wine maker to the property one night. The kid had actually grown up in a house adjacent to the vines. It was fun to have permission to go past the locked gate of the vineyard and see the interior of the place. A sort of idyllic setting to raise a child.

Anyway, I promise to have as many Uber cars at Roblar as possible at 10PM. This was on a Thursday, and the wedding was Saturday. I give the couple my card and ask them to call and confirm before Saturday. They assure me that they would call. The bride-to-be comments that they are especially interested in getting a ride for themselves. I promised that I personally would be there to insure they got to their hotel safely.

So, being a newish and naïve Uber driver, I text some other drivers about the event and ask them to spread the word. The responses back were sort of blasé and wisecracky. That was the first warning. The other drivers had been to a few of these rodeos and were nonplussed at the news of a 10PM Uber rush.

So Friday rolls around. No confirmation call. Then Saturday. No call. Now it is Saturday afternoon. I have a fare in the car, and as usual it was casual and loose conversation. I ask if I can share about my upcoming Uber dilemma and the couple is all ears (people love to hear any kind of Uber story). The series of events is explained to the fare. The dilemma is that 10PM Saturday night is prime time for Uber pickups. The restaurants are closing and many folks will be wanting to uber home. Fulfilling the commitment to the soon-to-be-married couple will require going **OFFLINE** at least an hour beforehand to insure no ride requests come in for a distant destination such as Santa Barbara. I then must drive to Roblar, wait for the reception to end, and hopefully locate the bride and groom to determine if they still need a ride. But since Bride and Groom have not confirmed the whole ordeal may be for naught.

The fare in the backseat have a definite opinion. *"You should go anyway. They were probably too busy with all the other wedding planning to think to call you."*

That is exactly what I'd been thinking. It was nice to get logic verification though. So a little after nine that night I went **OFFLINE** and headed to Roblar. If Bride and Groom had it right the Roblar parking lot should be deserted.

When I pulled in nearly every parking spot was taken. That was the second warning.

Bearing in mind the old expression 'In for a penny... in for a pound', I park the car and waited till exactly 10 o'clock. The party raging inside showed no signs of winding down. So I decide to do a recon and sauntered into the building. The first room encountered was a sort of mingling area with an open bar off to the left. To the right was an open set of double doors leading to what must have been the dance floor, given that music was pouring through the opening at about a thousand decibels. I walk through the doors. The room is full of drunk people dancing. I knew they were drunk because the band was horrible. The musicians were playing off-key and the sound being produced is technically undanceable. The dancers took no notice.

I spot Bride and Groom at the center of the dance floor. I decided to teach these people a lesson about following up words with actions. I leaned forward and stormed to the center of the room. Dancing couples scattered to avoid my headlong march. Bride and Groom were oblivious. I stepped between them, turned the bride toward me and slapped her. Hard. She spun around a few times then fell back into one of the chairs lining the wall. Tiny chirping birds began circling her head. The bridal bouquet flew into the next room and landed on the bartenders head. Before Groom could react I delivered a karate chop to his nose. As he fell back into a chair adjacent to his new wife I grabbed his champagne glass and finished the drink. The crowd was aghast. The crumpled up Bride and Groom were dazed and confused. The music stopped. I grabbed the microphone from the singer, turned to the crowd and exclaimed *"This is what happens to people who don't keep their promises."* There was an eternal pause that lasted a good three seconds, then the crowd began cheering and applauding. Clearly these friends and relatives of Bride and Groom had been on the receiving end of the couple's broken promises in the past. Without further ado I exited the building, got in my car, and went **ONLINE**.

Reader: "Uber James! Really?

Uber James: "No, not really"

Here's what actually happened when I entered the room: There were a few chairs in a dark corner and I used one. It's well after closing time at this point. A woman spots me and comes over. She asks if she can help me. Dressed in very non-wedding attire and feeling like a complete idiot I do my best to string enough words together at a sufficient volume level to make her understand my purpose for crashing the wedding. I basically tell her that I had promised the bride and groom a ride home, and wanted to know if they still need me. I stress that it is no problem at all if they have another ride home, but I was available if they still needed me. She seems to understand, tells me to wait there, and disappears through another set of double doors leading into what looked like a back room where the core wedding party was hanging out.

I never saw her again.

After a while Bride herself pops into the room from the inner sanctum. Her stance, if not her garb, announced that she was the center of attention as she flitted around the room for a moment apparently looking for something or somebody. She maneuvers around the perimeter of the dancers, eyeballs me in the corner, says nothing, flitters a bit longer then disappears through the opening she had emerged from.

I ponder as to whether what I'd just witnessed had anything to do with Uber and come up answerless. My ears are now bleeding from the music so the mission is assigned a status of **aborted**. I go back to the car and go ONLINE. *Somebody* is going to need a ride home and I'm just the man to give it to them. Within a few minutes people start pouring out the main entrance. They line up in two facing rows and make an arch for Bride and Groom to exit through. The newlyweds pass happily through. It's so much fun they do it again.

The driver app then lights up and it's a fare from Roblar needing a ride. How convenient. I pull the car up near the entrance and start scanning for someone looking like they're trying to spot an Uber car. The fare discovers the car and several people start loading up. People are milling around the area when suddenly Groom appears. He recognizes me, gives a big smile, and exclaims "Hey, you're the guy who picked us up the other day." I smile and nod affirmatively. He shakes my hand and moves on.

What did I say? Nothing. There was *nothing* to say. I couldn't very well scold him for being a flake. And clearly there were plenty of cars for him and Bride to get to wherever they were headed next. From Groom's perspective everything was going wonderfully. And that of course is what counted. Ahh, such is life in the service industry. It's the little people who always get shorted (hint: I like being a member of the little people. Less responsibility).

So with my fare all loaded up we set course for the Marriott Hotel. Now here's some karmic justice for you. The Marriott was only a 15 minute drive, but an Uber "surge" was in effect at that time of the evening, so I made $65 for what would have normally been a $15 fare. As Harcourt Fenton Mudd once said: "Oh you beautiful universe."

Uber Story   Uber Story   Uber Story

Uber James Gets Stood Up at the Altar - Occurrence B

At this point in time it's late September and wedding season is in full bloom. The word was that the season would peak in October. I got this indirectly from some wedding photographers, and they should know. What ever happened to the June bride? Well in the Santa Ynez Valley October is the new June. Not sure about elsewhere. Apparently people are trying to beat the heat. It's still good weather in October, and getting married in the valley this late in the year sort of folds into the grape harvest which happens in October as well. You have to pick those grapes when they're ripe.

This particular wedding story began unfolding on a Saturday afternoon. I pick up a fare at The Landsby in Solvang and learn there's a wedding taking place that evening at a combination horse ranch and vineyard named 'Bella Cavalli Farms'. This was special news because I'd been driving by the entrance to this place for weeks and had always wondered about it. The property occupies a swath of a giant section of bottomland running along Hwy 246 between Solvang and Buellton. The 2-lane road is lined with parallel rows of Monterey Cypress trees planted on the shoulders. This region of the valley is referred to by locals as 'The Flats'.

The property lines around the flats are partitioned off with wooden and barbed wire fences. It makes for quite the sight to drive through the flats and look past the Cypress trees to see the sun shining onto grassy fields full of horses and cattle.

Especially horses. Remember that horse ranching is a *really big deal* in the valley. There are many well-known equestrian related establishments here sporting international reputations. The flats were once owned entirely by 'Monte Roberts', who was described to me by my motel manager as a true 'horse whisperer', or as his website describes him, "*The Man Who Listens to Horses*". For the last fifty years Monte has drawn in horse lovers from around the world to visit his equestrian academy, as students and interns learn about his unique 'Join-up' training technique. The parcel now occupied by Bella Cavalli Farms was sold off by Monte about ten years ago. The farm is easy to spot from the Highway as it has a horse race track surrounded by grape vines. The vines grow both inside and outside the oblong track. Quite unique!

Land of many uses!

This is all very interesting but we have yet to reach the heart of the story. At one point in the day I had ferried the bride to the event location for some sort of pre-wedding party. The previous story notwithstanding it was actually rare to get the actual bride or groom in the car. Wedding party members, yes. But less often the folks actually tying the knot. I'm talking to the fare before this is revealed and happen to ask what the bride and groom are up to at the moment. A woman in the back informs me that the bride is sitting right behind me. Really?

Somebody mentions that the groom is *not* in the car, and the bride jokingly says "No. He's out and you're in James." Everybody laughs. I missed my line, which would have been something like a quote from the movie Weird Science, when a beautiful woman appears out of nowhere in front of two undeserving teenagers, and they respond; *"Thank you God!"* Oh well. The bride then issues the standard issue question:

Bride: "Where are you from Uber James?"

Uber James: "Big Sur."

Bride: "I LOVE Big Sur! I wanted to get married there, but we couldn't work out the logistics."

For the moment her comment meant little. The group arrives at their destination and slips out of the car. Later in the day it occurred to me that I had the perfect gift for the bride. Given what she had said about longing to have been married in Big Sur it seemed she might appreciate being gifted a 'Boogielight' at her wedding in Solvang. I mentioned these LED keychain flashlights in chapter 9 – Uber Tales From the Heart. The flashlight has a Big Sur logo on it.

Boogielight with Highway 1 keychain

I knew the wedding location but didn't want to just show up. The event was not due to take place for a few hours and it seemed a sneakier way could be found to slip the gift to someone in the wedding party. Soon afterwards the driver app lit up for a pickup at a Santa Ynez eatery. The car filled up with people heading to The Landsby. They mentioned a wedding they were attending shortly at Bella Cavalli Farms. It was *the* wedding. Of course I had no idea where these folks fit in. Was it the groom's side or the bride's? I gingerly asked if they knew the bride personally. No. They were with the groom. None-the-less I gave them an outline, which was the right thing to do because one gentleman in the car was the minister who was marrying the pair. He was all for taking possession of the Boogie-light and finding a way to give it to the bride.

I gave the minister one of the flashlights and then we were at The Landsby. He requested I take his group to the wedding later. I agreed and asserted that I wished to give him a card to accompany the gift. He was fine with that and told me to be back at the hotel at 7:45PM. He was quite adamant about the time. 7:45! He actually gave me a twenty dollar bill to insure the car would be waiting. Given that we are talking about a two mile, $5 Uber ride, the tip was quite generous.

I went OFFLINE in plenty of time to pick up Minister and company at the appointed hour. The Prius rolled into the driveway of The Landsby at 7:40.

At 8 o'clock I went into the lobby/lounge. The group was nowhere to be seen. Where did they go?? Never did find out. Who knows, maybe the bride will read this book someday and write to tell me if she ever got her Big Sur Boogie-light.

Uber Story   🚗   Uber Story   🚗   Uber Story

Let's Makes a Habit of it

Telling this short and simple story affords the opportunity to inform you of a popular winery and what is perhaps the most expensive place to get married in the valley; Sunstone Winery. I may have had more fares to/from Sunstone than any other winery. People seem to love the wine, and the proprietors sponsor a number of events on the property.

Separate from the winery, but at the same vineyard, is the 8,500 sq. ft. Sunstone Villa. What is it? It's an authentic villa, set on a hilltop overlooking 50 acres of vines, the winery, the east end of the valley, and the surrounding Santa Ynez Mountains. It's all very posh posh at the villa. Sunstone's website actually claims the building was "... built from imported limestone from a small village in France...."

There had been so many fares heading to weddings at this villa

I started to get curious as to how much it cost to host an event there. One evening while picking up a fare from the location I made friends with one of the event crew. I speculated, quite ignorantly, that the place must go for at least five grand. Turns out that number needed another zero. It's about $50K for a full-on catered weekend event.

At some point I had picked up a couple from the Wine Valley Inn & Cottages that had honeymooned at Sunstone some six years earlier. The couple had honeymooned at Sunstone some six years earlier. They had been making the pilgrimage back to the valley on their anniversary every year since. They seemed a happy couple.

Uber Story   Uber Story   Uber Story

It Was Mine to Lose… And I Nearly Did

Got a ride request one Saturday afternoon for a pickup in a residential area of Santa Ynez. I find the address and follow the meandering driveway up a short hill to the house. Standing in front of the house are two couples. Age-wise they are pushing toward thirty. Each is holding a beer. Before I can exit the vehicle and get their doors a male from the group comes right up to my window.

Male: "I've got a question."

Uber James: "OK."

Male: "Can we bring our beers?"

Uber James: "YES."

They pile in the car and we are off to the Kronborg Inn, where this smallish group was going to meet up with the rest of their gang, pile in a party bus, and head to a wedding. A close friend of theirs from the valley was getting married. These kids had all grown up here. I think it was my first locals wedding and was happy for it. It was enjoyable to meet the people that live in the valley year round.

So first let me address the question that's on your mind. *"Why did Uber James let people in his car with open containers?"* Good question. Here's my logic. I would have rather risked an open container bust in a car with a sober driver than to leave those people to their own devices, i.e., driving their own vehicles because they couldn't get a ride. Early on in my Uber career I had picked up two intoxicated girls from the Marriott Hotel. They were obnoxiously drunk and wanted to get to Santa Barbara before the State Street night clubs closed. That was a one hour trip. The ladies had me stop and wait at the Maverick Saloon in Santa Ynez while they grabbed a quick drink. The returned to the car with plastic cups full of booze. I said nothing. We jumped on the 154 and headed south to Santa Barbara.

That was the first time someone had entered the car with an open container and I had not yet formulated a policy. My biggest concern, quite frankly, was that one of the two might spill their drink, or worse yet, barf in my BRAND NEW CAR. The only rule I had firmly established at the time was No Barfing. Neither girl showed any signs of that. They were too busy being loud and obnoxious. It's when someone goes from loud to dead quiet that worry breaks out.

We made it to SB without incident. But afterwards I did some thinking on how best to handle a repeat occurrence. I actually spoke to a CHP officer at the Buellton Starbucks. The question posed was along the lines of a sober Uber driver being discovered to have passenger(s) with an open container. The reply was slightly ambiguous. It *is* illegal... because the Prius is not a limousine... which has a partitioned off drivers area... which makes it legal to have that open container in the back. But for the Prius it would be "the officer's discretion."

That was an honest answer that made sense. Clearly a stop of that nature would be about how well the driver was maintaining control of the vehicle. Were the passengers in any way interfering with the driver? Was the car being pulled over for swerving on the road? So my take was that if things looked cool a little leeway *might* be given. As it turned out, open container occurrences were *very* rare. The two or three times it did happen the passengers were responsible, which makes sense because they were smart enough to call for an Uber car in the first place.

Which was exactly the case with the crew I'm telling you about right now. They *asked* permission up front. They were not drunks. They were simply drinking that day in celebration. Furthermore I had sized them up as salt-of-the-earth ranch-style boys and girls. The guys had likely played football back in high-school (the local team is 'The Pirates'). The girls may well have been on the cheerleading squad. These kids were social A-listers. We weren't going to have a problem, and it was only five miles to the Kronborg. As it turned out Uber James was the only source of the tiny problem that *did* arise.

Pretty much everybody dreads seeing these buses coming

So we're on our way to Solvang and it's all happiness and sunshine. The front passenger seat was occupied by the guy who had quizzed me before the ride. He's telling me about how long he's been asking his girl to marry him, but she keeps saying no. To demonstrate he turns around and asks her right then.

Boyfriend: "Will you marry me?"

Girlfriend "Yes."

The guy explodes. For some reason he attributes her change of heart to me. "James! Dude! She never said yes before. You made it happen. Will you be my best man?"

I'm serious. He asked me to be his best man. I played along. *"Sure."*

Everyone in the car is howling. Then the conversation shifts to another topic and turns inward, meaning the group was talking among themselves and Uber James was not a part of it. We get to Solvang and there is this nasty backup on the 246. We're stuck in traffic. This stuckness continues for a few minutes. I start to become concerned my fare is going to miss their bus. I'm thinking that since these guys had grown up here they may know a shortcut. In the back the conversation has built up to a frenzy... people talking in succession with no pause. There is no possibility of sliding in a question. I lose patience and interrupt (Big Mistake). In a tone more serious and taunting then intended, I shout out to the male in back who is talking the loudest "Excuse me Mr. I-grew-up-in-Santa-Ynez. Do you think we should try to find a shortcut?" The inside of the car goes dead silent.

Mr. I-grew-up-in-Santa-Ynez: "Don't F*** it up James"...... "Don't F*** it up."

He must have said this four or five times. His girlfriend injects that they have plenty of time before the bus leaves and that all is well.

The mood in the car has unwound. I shut my mouth and keep it that way for the reminder of the trip. Slowly the conversation builds up again. When I let the kids off at the Kronborg it's all smiles and thank yous. And my new friend in the front seat wants me to drive them from the wedding to the Maverick Saloon later. But that earlier out-of-place exchange sure had taken the edge off. Not a deal breaker by any means, but as the gentleman in the back seat walked away from the car he looked my way with a short, restrained smile. I knew from his look I had stung his sensibilities, and of course when someone has had a few beers such a faux pas is compounded.

As it happens the party bus took the wedding attendee's to the Maverick and I did not see that crew again. The guy who was now engaged was thoughtful enough though to text me the change in plans. I have to wonder if that couple really did get married. I had a sense that the reason the girlfriend was holding back was that the guy maybe still had a bit of a wild streak in him. But he looked like a good man, and I should have suggested to her to just marry him and have a baby early on, as fatherhood would bring her new husband down to earth.

Or maybe saying nothing at all was best.

THIRTEEN

NO UBER FOR YOU! COME BACK...
THREE DAYS

High Strangeness in the Santa Ynez Valley

What do you think?

Situation Resolved

Waxing Philosophically

*"Just because you're paranoid doesn't mean people
aren't out to get you."*
-Adapted from a Joseph Heller quote

High Strangeness in the Santa Ynez Valley

At one point while staying in the Santa Ynez Valley I lost my privilege to drive for Uber. I went to go **ONLINE** one morning and was unable to do so. A generic error message stated the there was a "problem" with my account. A problem? What could this be? I emailed Uber support but the only additional information reported was that a complaint was under investigation. How could this be? I had not the slightest problem with a fare in recent memory.

It would be three days before the problem was resolved, at the cost of $500 in lost revenue and a bit of shock and awe. To properly explain what happened we need to back up about three weeks before this event. I had taken a fare from Buellton to the Santa Barbara airport. There is no Trader Joe's grocery store in the valley so I decided to hit one of the several TJ's in SB. After passing through the checkout stand I visited the little boy's room prior to exiting the store. I then set course for a return to Solvang. Of course I *had* to stop at the famous In-N-Out Burger for a delicious hamburger. I place my order, go through the line, and upon retrieving my wallet to pay for the burger discovered that said wallet was missing in action.

My wallet was gone! And the ashtray I normally keep full of quarters in all my cars for just such an emergency was not helpful, because the Prius doesn't have an ashtray. All cash and credit cards were in the wallet. There wasn't even enough gas in the tank to get home. I always could go to a relative's house in

SB for money, but upon retracing my steps it hit me that the wallet was likely at Trader Joe's.

I call TJ's. Yep. They had it at the service counter. A customer had turned it in. Truthfully I wasn't surprised. Why? I've mentioned my theory that everyone is sort of "magnetized" in some way. We all have things we tend to draw and things we tend to repel. Plenty of things come to me that I'd prefer didn't, but one thing I've always drawn that's helpful is getting back items that are lost or stolen. For example one time I lost my wallet in the woods of Montana near Glacier National Park, yet upon returning to the hotel the wallet was waiting at the front desk. My family had been freaking a bit, but I felt it would be ok. And it was. This is not to be arrogant. I was most appreciative of the universe facilitating the wallet's return.

As I was this time. I zoomed back to TJ's, repossessed the wallet, and tried to dispense a reward to the honest customer who had found it on the floor in the bathroom. Alas, they were long gone. So that was that. Now fast forward three weeks. I get a request to retrieve two travelers from an Airbnb deep in Santa Ynez. It was a single-family residence with a number of other buildings on the property, including a barn, horse corrals, and a guest house. This is not an unusual configuration in Santa Ynez. And like others in the valley the family was garnering some extra income by renting out their guest house to tourists.

I pulled the Prius up in front of the main house, and not knowing the location of the guest quarters signaled the fare to meet me there. The day was warming, so while waiting I took my vest off. I placed my wallet from the vest on top of the car FOR 30 SECONDS while storing the vest in the back. I opened the hatchback, threw the vest in, closed the hatchback, and got back in the car.

Yep. That's right. I had instantly forgotten about the wallet. So now my fare is coming down the drive. I get the two ladies secured in the car and off we go to Beckman Vineyards for the drop off. Hours later I need my wallet to pay for something at the store, and it's gone. Uh oh. My first thought was that losing my wallet twice in one month might be too much for the lost item fairies that usually help me out. I was really pressing my luck.

Again I retrace my steps and discover that the last resting place of the wallet was on the roof of the Prius. Stupid. Stupid. Stupid. This was not going to be an easy retrieval. How far had the car gone before the wallet flew off? Difficult to say. The house where I picked up my fare was in an extremely quiet neighborhood. The street was only about a lane and a half wide, and it was a dead end. That was all favorable. I doubted that the wallet lasted much longer than where the lane turned onto the main road. I started looking at that intersection assuming that the centrifugal force at the corner would have thrown the wallet clear if it had been still clinging to the roof at that point.

A twenty minute search of the area turned up nothing. The next step was to search the lane leading to the pickup point. The distance was about a half a mile, and after slowly canvassing the area by car –with no results- I ended up exploring the street on foot over a period of several days. I would walk a section of the road until a ride request came in, then return sometime later and continue. There was no real hurry. For one thing, if the universe was going to deal me back my wallet it would do so. There was no need to get in a panic. You have to kind of let the magic happen. Plus, after the TJ's incident I had pulled one credit card out of the wallet and

stashed it in the center console, along with tips as they accumu-
lated. So I wasn't completely screwed.

To tell you the truth, I didn't even feel 100% comfortable
searching for the wallet past that initial recon in the car. It was
kind of *pushing* on the situation, rather than letting it percolate
on its own. That may not make sense, but life has taught me
when you push too hard things break. And indeed, I would
later pay for my obsessiveness.

Over the course of the next few days I explored further and
further down the lane, checking thoroughly in the many
shrubs lining the street, which took some time. No results. On
one occasion after rooting around for a while I felt tired. I
hadn't gotten enough sleep the night before and it was
catching up. So I simply sat in the car with the seat tilted back
and snoozed for about twenty minutes. It was a very quiet
street, I had seen only the odd neighbor walking their dog, so
felt quite comfortable sneaking a nap on the shoulder of
the road.

I woke up groggy and decided not to search any more that day.
I swung the Prius onto the road and headed back to the intersection. As I approached the intersection an ambulance,
followed by a huge Santa Barbara County fire truck, was
turning into the lane. "Wow. I wonder what's going on?" As the
ambulance passes me the female driver stops. I stop. She leans
out the window and says "Were you just sleeping in your car a
few minutes ago?" Uh oh. "Yes", I reply. "Well this is all for
you." Yikes. "Sorry." She has nothing further to say so I
speed away.

Gee whiz I sure am sorry to put y'all out like that. But I was
only napping! I concluded that rather than come up and tap on
the window of a stranger's car, one of the neighbors had simply

called it in. That was understandable. It's nice to know that if I had been in trouble there would have been help.

So now fast forward another few days. I've just returned to the valley after a quick trip home to Big Sur when the smoke had waned for a few days. There was some computer work for a client that needed tending to, and I wanted to see if someone had found the wallet and mailed it to the address on my driver's license. No one had, nor had anyone called to report they had found the wallet.

While at home I had grabbed an old wallet and an expired driver's license. I've now returned to Santa Ynez and have ventured back into the neighborhood that's hopefully still harboring the lost wallet. This is going to sound silly but I retrieved the spare wallet to perform a test. I drove to the Airbnb and placed the wallet on top of the Prius to see how long it would take for it to fly off as the car drove down the lane. It slid off the car in a matter of yards. This was at a final 50 ft. section of thick bushes leading up to the house my fare had come. It was the only section that had not yet been searched. Once that search was complete I was going to give up. It sounds counter-intuitive but I had not canceled my credit cards. This was purposeful. Keeping credit cards active in such cases is a marker as to whether someone had found the wallet. Consumers are not on the hook if someone fraudulently uses a lost card so the risk is low. The first email indicating a charge had been made on any of the cards would have indicated someone of dubious reputation had found the wallet and that it was not likely to be returned. Of course the credit cards would then be immediately reported lost.

Before commencing the search I walked to the Airbnb house that the fare had stayed at and knocked on the door. A teenager answers the door. I introduce myself, explain the situation, and offer my card in case they find the wallet. The young man accepts the card and nods affirmatively. Sure, contact could have been made earlier but I had suspected all along that the wallet had at least had made it clear of the driveway before flying away. But now leads were getting sparse.

The search of the last set of bushes takes maybe half an hour and produces no fruit. There was nothing left to do except either wait for the wallet to magically make its way back into my hands, or replace its contents. Either way, time spent in this neighborhood had drawn to an end. While driving back toward the intersection two spectacles draw my attention. One is a cluster of people about 50 feet ahead on the left, standing at the end of their driveway. Perhaps a woman and a couple of children. There may or may not have been a male. I barely registered them. What diverted my attention was the police car that had just turned down the lane. "Huh", I think. "Something amiss in the neighborhood?" Proceeding down the narrow lane I give plenty of easement to the cop car, but he is not returning the favor. We reach an impasse so I stop my car on the shoulder. He stops his car, blocking me. I remain in the Prius. He gets out of his vehicle and walks right to me.

Uber James: "Hello. I was just trying to get down the street... unless you're here for me...??

Cop: "I'm here for you."

The officer conducts a short interview. He wants to know what I'm doing on the street. I inform him that I drive for Uber and lost my wallet nearby when retrieving a fare. Now a second cop car turns into the lane and parks behind the first car. There are two cops in that car. They are all deputy sheriffs. I will refer to the three deputies by size, which was medium, large, and extra-large. The deputy speaking to me, officer Large, has gone over to the people standing in their driveway. The other two cops, both males, join the party. I remain seated. The cops confer for a moment and then the pair from the second car come over. Officer extra-large stands a few yards away from the Prius at about 10 o'clock to my position. He is fully in my view. Officer medium takes up a defensive position just behind the driver's door of the Prius. He's leaning right up against the car for cover, one hand close to his holster.

Santa Barbara Sheriffmobile on the job

I've seen enough cops shows to know that the stance taken by both officers is to protect their lives. I had to crane around to get a look at the cop next to the car, whereas he could look straight into the car at me and see where my hands were. In the meantime the cop in the street had a clear shot at me. I'm not saying I was worried about that. I'm just saying they were taking precautions. I understood, and was not offended at their posturing. After all, they *could* have yanked me from the car and placed me spread-eagle face down on the pavement. So the Deputies were being pretty cool, relatively speaking. I would have preferred to exit the car and have a face to face discussion with both the cops and the people who had apparently called them in, but those days have been gone for many years.

Officer medium: "Hey, what's up?"

Uber James: "I'm not sure how to answer that. Do you have a question?

Officer medium: "Well my Sergeant there (pointing to officer Large talking to the homeowners) told me to come over and find out what's going on.

I decided to take him at his word, foregoing the possibility he was trying to engage in some kind of cat and mouse game. I gave him full cooperation and answered all his questions, even the ones I wasn't legally obliged to. I told him the whole story about Uber, the lost wallet, my luck at getting lost items back, and my insistence on canvassing the area thoroughly before giving up (*it didn't occur to me to mention that today was the final search outing*).

Both officers have been listening to all this with a standard issue look of unwavering suspicion on their faces. They reminded me of how a hawk gambits that its shadow continually cast on the ground below will sooner or later flush its prey. The deputies showed no signs of buying my story, but neither did they seem to conclude I was likely a mass murderer hiding in the bushes till nightfall.

There was some further questioning regarding if I had any registered firearms, had I ever been arrested, so on and so forth. I had good answers to all the questions and was able to provide the vehicle registration, proof of insurance, and even a picture ID (the expired license). I was pretty clean.

The cops confer again and this time Officer Large (the

sergeant) comes over. Keep in mind that the concerned home-owners, ostensibly the ones who called 911, are now fully briefed as to why the stranger has been coming into the neighborhood. There is in fact a reason this older single man had been repeatedly visiting the street and nosing around in the bushes.

Officer Large tells me that the family apologized for calling the police on me, and now that it had been determined why the stranger was hanging around they were all going to help me out. Mom. Dad. Kids. Everyone. "We'll find your lost wallet!"

Actually, that's *not* what happened. What happened was the cop told me the people wanted me to leave and never come back. He pointed out that the street we were on is actually private, and marked thusly. He adds "They said they would get in touch if they find your wallet." Uh huh.

So now Officer large retreats back to the family and Officer Medium takes charge again. He politely inquires what I'm planning on doing now. I had no choice but to go along with the homeowner's wishes. As I later learned, the street was indeed private. Many streets in the valley are. It's a byproduct of larger parcels of land being subdivided over the decades. They had cut roads to all the subdivided parcels but the easements remained in private hands. So I told the deputy I would respect the people's wishes to not return and that I would go about replacing the contents of the wallet, starting with my driver license, which I was politely informed technically left me illegal to drive.

The cops liked my plan.

What do you think?

I have to wonder what readers think of this story so far. It seems to me one could take either side of the argument. On the one hand Uber James was quietly going about looking for a very important lost object. Especially when you factor in identity theft. There had never been a conversation, a confrontation, an exchange of hard looks, nor even eye contact with the home owners. I didn't know I was being observed!

On the other hand who could blame the homeowners for not simply coming out and asking what I was up to? The man of the house may not have been home, and there were the children to think of. I had come into the neighborhoods several times. And when you consider the prior ambulance incident, my presence there probably looked pretty weird.

So, my feathers were ruffled but I really couldn't fault the 911 callers. And although the cops showed no signs of having advocated on my behalf, they could have been a lot tougher on me. They *could* have towed my car, since technically I couldn't drive without a valid license.

The story's not over though. Now let's get back to when I was telling you about how I couldn't go online. This is the day after tangling with the police, which was a Thursday. So I'm **OFFLINE** all day Friday, clueless as to why. I made no connection whatsoever with the prior day's events. Saturday morning comes and still no word from Uber. Saturday evening an email finally comes in, but it's time stamped Friday at 12:30AM. That was nearly a full day earlier. Weird. Something has delayed the email. The message is from Uber and relates to why I'm offline. Uber is inquiring as to whether I've have had any problems with fares recently. They are fishing. I reply back stating that there have been no issues other than not being able to go **ONLINE**! In short order I receive another Uber email. They are asking permission to call me. Of course!

You must understand that other than periodic drop-in meetings at a local Uber office there is no way for a driver to converse with Uber live. No phone calls. No live texting. Only a submission form on the website. So it was gratifying to be able to speak with someone on the phone. The call came within a few minutes...

Uber rep: "Do you recall giving a ride at such and such address in Santa Ynez?"

The rep was referring to the Airbnb pick up where I lost my wallet!

Uber James: "Yes"

Uber rep: "We have a report of an Uber driver behaving inappropriately after the fare."

Uber James: "Oh my god. That report could not have come from the fare. They are long gone. Someone else must have filed a complaint."

Yeah. "Someone" else had. The rep did not offer the complainant's name, and I knew enough not to ask. I was shocked at the reveal and explained how I had lost my wallet and had been combing the neighborhood for it. That was the reason I had been behaving *inappropriately*. Fortunately the rep was a sharp guy and got it. He said he would take the information back to his "team" and that I would be hearing back shortly. The Uber rep also added that in cases having anything to do with safety, the driver is taken offline while an investigation is held.

Situation Resolved

Sometime the following morning I'm able to back **ONLINE**. I calculated that the downtime had cost me an estimated $500 in weekend earnings.

What is one to think of *this* event? I had to assume that the family who called the police on me had called Uber later that day as well. But why? They had gotten what they wanted earlier. The stranger had promised not to return to the neighborhood. They had gotten full cooperation with absolutely no sass. Why not let it go? Especially since I had demonstrated a reason for being in the area. And again, there had been no close encounters. I was never even near their property line. Their children had not walked by while I was searching, I was clearly not a vagrant. In fact, I was driving a BRAND NEW CAR. Hello?! What were you thinking?

I'll never know what those folks were thinking. I suspect they were one of the many SoCal transplants that have migrated to the valley seeking a simpler lifestyle. I don't think someone who grew up in a low-key community like Santa Ynez would have reacted like that. Perhaps the family moved from an area with a high crime rate. From their point of view there was this dude who kept coming into their neighborhood who didn't belong. Still, they had won the battle so why contact Uber? That strikes me as unreasonable fear, and there's a name for that.

Waxing Philosophically

The thing about paranoia is that it can produce the exact result you are trying to avoid. After the incident a part of me was feeling quite trespassed upon. Thoughts of vengeance came to mind. And the family had shown themselves! Why if you are concerned that there's a creepy person in the neighborhood, do you come outside and tacitly inform the perp it was you who called the police?? In their fear they were not thinking and had made themselves vulnerable.

I did not obey the voice urging retribution. This was a clear case of when the putting-others-first philosophy discussed in Chapter 11 can and should be applied. I'm grateful to have had the presence of mind to do so. Twenty years earlier and that may not have been the case.

In spite of the hurt feelings I can't judge that family. As much as I would have loved hating them for costing me time, money, and worry, I don't know what their point of view was. So often in life, situations *appear* one way, but when the time is taken to learn the facts, things are actually quite different. Appearances really can be deceiving. This is why they stopped hanging supposed horse thieves way back when.

And for all I know those aren't even the people who contacted Uber. It's highly likely it was them, but it *could* have been the family whose house I dropped my card off at. Or perhaps some other neighbor. I'm told by locals that people in the valley value their privacy. At the end of the day I just let go of the whole incident and that was that.

The Three Axioms of Life

Have you ever heard of the Three Axioms of Life? They are:

1. Shit happens

2. Bring beer

3. Don't be stupid

After the lost wallet event I thought of petitioning the fictitious organization that maintains the axioms. I wanted to add an additional axiom:

4. Don't put shit on top of your car

I told a fare about the suggested 4th axiom. They said don't bother making the request because the action actually comes under axiom 3.

FOURTEEN
A DAY IN THE LIFE OF AN UBER DRIVER

21 Rides

"I've got to admit it's getting better. It's a little better all the time."
- Paul McCartney

21 Rides

What is a typical day in the life of a fulltime Uber driver? You might as well ask what's a typical day in the life of a random number. But here's how it went on the very day this driver thought to include such a topic in this book. This particular day would find five skateboards making their way into the hatchback of the Prius, the biggest man in the world taking a ride, Uber James receiving a hug, later a kiss, and it would rain for the first time in... forever. This all happened on October 16th, 2016, at which point the forest fire smoke had fully retreated from the valley and the air was fresh and clean.

First thing that morning was a trip to the Buellton McDonalds for a large coffee and an oatmeal. This had become a daily routine. I try to avoid fast food in general, but in my view McDonalds makes a better cup of coffee than Starbucks, and it's only a buck for a large. You have to get it fresh though. They served me a stale cup one day so I asked the attendant how long McDonalds lets a pot sit before tossing it. She replied two hours and grimaced. *Two* hours? You gotta watch these people every second. The oatmeal cup, while perhaps not as healthy as what one might make at home, is a tasty and relatively wholesome and inexpensive way to start the day, and the container fit right into one of the coffee cup holders in the car. This allowed me to sip my coffee and pick at my breakfast as I ran morning errands such as washing the car, buying water, or doing laundry. One item on the task list today was to send a note to Uber informing them that after several weeks, the laminated Uber signs for the car still hadn't shown up. The driver app would be running while the list was checked off in case a local needed a ride to work. Most tourists didn't need a ride until maybe mid-morning.

Here's how the day unfolded:

Ride #1: Took a chef who cooks at a top restaurant in Santa Ynez to work.

Ride #2: Picked up a local girl who doesn't drive. She usually wants to go to Albertson's for groceries or to Starbucks for a latte. Today it was Starbucks and back again.

Ride #3: Picked up a local in Solvang who works at Paula's Pancake House in Buellton. I love Paula's and am always happy to shuttle the employee back and forth to work. It's an opportunity go in and sneak a bite.

Ride #4: Drove two locals from Los Olivos to retrieve their vehicle from a bar they had left it at the night before.

There is a lull in ride requests so I go back to my motel and finish breakfast sitting at one of the tables in the open court-yard. I had started the book by now and was writing a bit each day on a laptop. As so often happens the motel manager, Johnny, catches a break in his morning duties and we launch into one of our typical conversations, which includes random observations on human behavior, paths to enlightenment, the frustrations of maintaining a high-minded attitude when dealing with tourists and traffic (we each got our turn), and how things are in China (Johnny's parents are from China and he grew up in the valley. He had spent a few years in the home-land recently to learn the language better).

Then the driver's app lights up and we go our separate ways.

Ride #5: A three hour Uber Wine tour.

Ride #6: I take a private pilot and his wife to the tiny Santa Ynez airport. It's fairly common for pilots to use Uber to shuttle to/from the airport. This was an unusual fare because the man had built the plane he was flying. He called it an *experimental* plane. I took photos but somehow they are gone. Too bad.

Ride #7: First of two trips to Santa Barbara (not terribly unusual). Picked up two 30-something ladies from a fund raiser for a non-profit related to helping kids in foster homes. The event had been held at Sunstone Winery. One of the gals admitted she had drank a bit too much wine. She in particular is very talkative the whole way down. Good person though. We get deep into philosophy of life stuff. She gives me a giant hug goodbye.

Ride #8: While in Santa Barbara did a pickup at The Hyatt on the beach. Probably one or two other pickups. Can't recall details. Then headed up Hwy 101 back to Buellton.

Ride #9: A couple wants to get to the remotely located Sanford winery before the tasting room closes. We zoom and make it in time.

Ride #10: It's dark now. Picked up a couple at the Hitching Post. They had come to the valley on a Harley. The man sat in front. He may have been the biggest dude I've ever seen in person. He was on crutches from a knee operation. I honestly don't know how he fit in the front seat.

Ride #11: Picked up a nasty looking blonde in Buellton and delivered her to Solvang. The pickup address came through as somewhere on Hwy 246, no numeric, and the only thing at the

GPS coordinates was... *Hwy 246*. Finally located her. She was fully toasted. Kissed my hand when she got out and said good bye.

Ride #12: Another trip to Santa Barbara. Picked up two teenage boys from the exclusive 'Dunn School'. They needed to get to the train station in SB by 9:30PM. We loaded their two skateboards in the back. The young gentlemen made it in plenty of time. Stayed in SB for a while.

Ride #13: Picked up three lovely 20-something girls from a chic eating spot called 'The Lark' in Santa Barbara's hip *Funk Zone*. Delivered them to a condo in the upscale town of Montecito, just south of SB. One girl asks for an Uber story. Another injects *"And no stories about having sex in the back seat of your car!"* I tell her the story of giving a Boogie-light to the five year old (Chapter 9).

Ride #14: Another Funk Zone pickup, this time from Figueroa Mountain Brewing Company. A couple from New York. They were going back to this incredible boutique hotel cloistered way up in the SB hills. The dude was smart. He worked for a luxury car company and was telling me about how they were trying to work a deal with Uber to provide cars to Uber drivers. He mentions that in his locale, the pool of Uber drivers is utilized at an average rate of 60%, whereas the utilization of the taxicab pool is 35%.

Ride #15: Picked up a gentleman and drove him to the gas station he worked at in order to turn in his graveyard shift.

Ride #16: Picked up another gentleman standing alone on lower State St. (downtown) in front of a construction area. Who knew where he had come from. He just wanted a ride home.

Ride #17: Back to the Funk Zone. Three huge skateboards find their way into the back, and the owners, three 20-somethings from Santa Clarita, just want a short ride to their hotel. The three hipsters had rolled from the hotel down to the FZ, but now the streets were wet with rain and their rides didn't have fenders.

Ride #18: Now it was time to respond to a ride request from three ladies who had completed their evening's events downtown and wanted to get back to the Fess Parker Resort. They have an uneventful trip to their hotel.

Ride #19: This was one of two bad rides that day. Bad rides are rare. I get a request for a pickup at a residential address. No one is there when I arrive. The phone rings. It's the fare. They got the pickup and destination addresses reversed. I say no problem, I drive to the other address and don't start the meter until the group is picked up. Four sullen passengers enter the car. I show my Uber screen to the girl who ordered the ride just to demonstrate that I didn't go to the wrong address. She ignores my invitation. The passengers are rude and lippy. Later that night my average star rating drops. Go figure.

Ride #20. (Aka Nightmare on Park Lane) Probably the only time Uber James got lost. A teen-age party was breaking up deep deep deep in the hills of posh Montecito. The serious money lives in there. By day the hills look sunny and beautiful, dotted with quaint country roads punctuated by wooden street signs. By night it's a funhouse gone wrong with impossibly narrow lanes, zero street lights, difficult to read street signs, and Eucalyptus fronds scatted across the road from a mysterious wind storm that just kicked off. Montecito turns into Creepville and the GPS isn't working. After going around the same loop of streets three times I call the fare and tell him I'm looking at two street signs with the same street name, pointing in opposite directions. The fare has no clue and after several tries explaining I'm out. I cancel the fare. The driver app then repeatedly lights up with requests from all the other party participants at the same address, as mine is the closest Uber car. I go offline and fight my way out of the jungle to let another car tag in. Perhaps they will have better luck.

Ride #21: It's getting toward midnight and I always knock off by then. Going north I grab a fare going to a condo a couple of freeway exits north. Then it's home to Solvang and off to bed.

FIFTEEN
UBER TALES FROM SANTA BARBARA

Uber Stories:
Four Tipsy Santa Barbara Blondes Returning Home From Wine Country
Zero Customer Service
Wait a minute. Where am I going?
Getting a Leg Up On the Competition
One Way to Pay for College
Caught in a Catch-22
The Woman Who Needed a New Friend
College Kids Overwhelm the Uber Network
Speaking of UCSB
If You Love Her Then You Must ...

"When I moved to Santa Barbara twenty years ago I was told to never get in argument with someone in traffic because you may be standing behind them at the grocery store checkout line the following day."
-Uber James

There are many reasons folks shuttle back and forth between the Santa Ynez Valley and the nearest city, Santa Barbara. It has the closest airport capable of handling large jets. Santa Barbara also has a train station connecting to more lines than the micro-Amtrak station in Lompoc. Tourists will often stay in Santa Barbara and do day trips to wine country. Valley locals will often escape to Santa Barbara to take in a show or shop the famous downtown district on State Street. We've been to SB in the Uber car several times so far in this book and here are a few more stories that may interest you.

Uber Story   🚗   Uber Story   🚗   Uber Story

Four Tipsy Santa Barbara Blondes Returning Home From Wine Country

This trip happened fairly soon after I hit the valley. Four 30-something married-with-children Santa Barbara women have this little clique where they depressurize from day-to-day life by periodically escaping to some kind of adventure. Kind of reminded me of the movie City Slickers, only with the genders reversed. When I caught up with these girls in Santa Ynez they had a full day of activities under their belts and needed a ride home. Yes, they had smartly left their cars back in SB and had Ubered the hour or so journey up to wine country.

The gals pour themselves into the car. We have a fun ride down the 154. The talk and the music are flowing freely. Suddenly we are forced to a complete stop. Nighttime highway construction. It works out that our car is at the head of the line. A mere few yards in front of the vehicle is a massive construction lighting fixture on a tripod. It illuminates the immediate area with a stark, surreal look. Cars start lining up behind us. In no time there is a string of headlights to the horizon.

My passengers have had enough of being cooped up in the car. *"Let's dance"*, says one of them. The doors fly open and the girls soar from the car. They flow behind the Prius and start dancing. No inhibitions. Dozens of eyeballs are focusing on the action. I turn the music up full blast.

It was a shame though. No other car doors opened. Virtually everyone else stayed behind closed doors. What rule exists that prevents so many, when given the opportunity to act like.... children... free spirits... they pass? This was a no risk opportunity on a warm dry evening to just cut loose for a minute. My four passengers were showing the way to fun!

You see people break out in dance in musicals like 'Across the Universe' and 'Grease'. But it's hard for many to express the wonder of life in real life. Here's an idea for a college paper for someone on the sociology track. Go around the world and create the above set of circumstances in every country you visit. Use whatever indigenous transportation exists. How would the scene play out in each of those cultures?

Zero Customer Service

Here's a good one. To set a context I would like to first say that at some point in life it occurred to me that there are two kinds of people in the world:

> *People who believe their own BS ...*
> *and the ones that know better.*

Do you hear me brothers and sisters? You see it's one thing to deceive. We all deceive at times. But when you actually start believing the deception that you yourself manufacture, well then you've got something special going. It's a trap any of us can fall into and we see examples every day. Of course we can always spot when someone *else* has drunk their own Kool-Aid. Self-delusion may be as common as its cousin: Denial. And as we all know, *denial ain't just a river in Egypt.*

Case in point: I pick up a single professional looking woman at the upscale Hadsten House hotel. The fare had mistakenly fingered the hotel next door as the pickup point. I find her anyway, and upon starting the trip the app reveals we are going to Santa Barbara. The well-dressed lady is on her way to a business meeting. She is somewhat quiet and reserved. The Prius gets on the 101 heading south. She gets on the phone. She's on the phone the entire 50 minute trip down. There are two objectives. Get the charges reversed for a SB hotel she had reserved but failed to show up at last night. And number two, find a hotel for tonight.

Something had gone wrong with the reservation at the Santa

Barbara hotel. Now she wants her credit card refunded. She's on the phone to the hotel, slowly working her way through the staff to accomplish her goal. They don't want to issue a refund. She reaches the top of the management ladder and finds a **No** waiting there too. My fare had been designated a no-show on the reservation, the credit card had guaranteed the room, so the room sat vacant all night. It shakes out that the woman had intended to reserve the room for tonight but mistakenly booked the previous night.

The business woman had started off quite calmly in her mission but is slowly getting worked up. *"How can you people treat your customers like this?"* That kind of thing. I must add that at no point did the woman present a scintilla of evidence that the fault was with the hotel. The reservation was on record, it simply had been made for the wrong day. The hotel has an airtight case against the woman.

So now she falls back to a *"Then at least give me ½ credit"* demand. The hotel doesn't budge. Then she starts lying about the circumstances to get out of paying the bill. Nothing works. As a last gambit she plays the public relations card. *"I messed up, but it is good PR for the hotel to wave the charge this one time."* No go.

The woman finally has to admit defeat. And to make matters worse the hotel has no space for her tonight. She moves on to finding a room elsewhere in Santa Barbara on a Friday night. Not a pleasant proposition. She finally finds a room but has to pay through the nose for it. Before moving on she sums up the ordeal by uttering in disgust *"Zero Customer Service."*

OK. What do you think about that one dear reader? I related the story to another fare. What did they think? All four thought the woman was out of line with her attitude. However, when asked if given the same circumstances would they try for the refund, I got back a chorus of yeses.

I suspect the logic there is that the hotel is in a much better position to weather the lost revenue than the consumer can afford to pay for an expensive service that goes unutilized. Therein lies the rationale for saying anything to get out of the bill. I suppose if her logic was phrased in verse it might look like this"

Here's a newsbreak
i take the cake
a word to the wise
i ration-a-lize
the rules won't apply
if i let out a Facebook cry
y'all better blink
or i'll make you extinct

But this hotel wasn't going for it. To its credit it held the line. Management stuck to its guns despite what the threat of a social media blitz of badmouthing might do to its image. What the hotel had going for it is that downtown Santa Barbara hotels are something of a sellers' market. It's a low-growth city and room occupancy rates often run to 100% on weekends.

But at the end of the day what struck me was how convinced the lady was that the hotel that was in the wrong. It doesn't hurt to go with the please-refund-me ploy, but don't forget whose mistake it was.

Uber Story   🚗   Uber Story   🚗   Uber Story

Wait a minute. *Where* am I going?

Here's a good example of the Uber uncertainty principle at work. The app lights up one evening just after dark with a pickup request for Industrial Eats in Buellton. I zoom straight for the restaurant (but never more than 5 over). Just out of the gate however the phone rings. It's the fare.

Man's voice: "We're not actually at the restaurant. We're at the hotel. We left the baby bag at the restaurant. Can you please retrieve it and bring it to us here"?

Uber James: "Of course. See you in a few minutes."

Ah ha. A mission. That is how I saw this ride. To paraphrase the famous cartoon hero Underdog: *"There's no need to fear... Ubercar is here."* I arrive at Eats, park, run in and ask at the counter for the bag. A girl behind the counter positively lights up when I identify myself. "It's so awesome that you're bringing them their bag!!" She scurry's to where the bag's been carefully stashed for safekeeping behind the counter and hands it off to me. I return the huge smile she is still sporting but am perplexed as to why it seems like such a big deal. The Marriott's only five minutes from here. And I *am* getting paid.

I scoot out the door, into the car, and out the driveway. The Marriott was my best guess as to what the gentleman meant by "the hotel" as it is one of the few nearby accommodations in Buellton that bills the property as a *hotel* over a motel or Inn.

But when I start the trip the app reveals the destination is in fact the Hotel Milo... which is near the beach in **Santa Barbara**.

Ha ha ha. That was why the server at the restaurant was so pleased. The family had apparently been day tripping up to the valley in their own car and had walked out of Eats without the baby gear. I then recalled that I had heard a baby crying in the background while speaking to the father. As so often happened an on-demand ride service saved the day. For those of you who recall Underdog's other mantra: *"When delivering pampers I am not slow... it's hip hip hip and away I go."*

(You really have to hear Underdog say it)

Note: For you millennials out there who maybe haven't had a taste of 60's cartoons you really should look up some Underdog episodes online. One of the better cartoon shows of its time.

Uber Story   🚗   Uber Story   🚗   Uber Story

Getting a Leg Up On the Competition

Here's another example of the voyeur aspect of being an Uber driver. In this context the term simply refers to listening in on the conversation the fare has going. It's pretty impossible not to, but as with the earlier story of the woman trying to get out of paying her hotel bill, I was riveted to the conversation taking place on this ride. The pickup was at the Fess Parker Inn, a large and luxurious resort right on the beach. The hotel has extensive convention facilities and because of its location and the panache associated with the city of Santa Barbara it's a popular booking destination for business conferences.

There was a weeklong convention being sponsored by a national online presence firm for its clients. One of the attendees explained that the firm had decided that rather than fly its sales force all around the country to visit clients, the company instead extended an annual invitation to bring its clients together in a single location. And where better to have such a *schmoose-fest* than beautiful Santa Barbara.

Most of the schmoozing I was witness to took place enroute to various lunch and dinner spots around town. Santa Barbara is known for its many great restaurants. So I was picking up a car full of passengers from the hotel and taking them to a restaurant... then back again. Lunch. Dinner. Here. There. But it was all sort of standard issue schmoozing techniques being deployed.

Until one afternoon there's a Fess Parker sourced ride request from two women. They aren't going to lunch. They are going for a *spa*. At the gorgeous Bacara Resort, a posh, upscale Spanish style resort famous for its spa facilities and isolated location on the Gaviota coast... a full twenty minute ride north.

These women are going to fit right in at the resort. The two are drop-dead beautiful, immaculately coiffed, fully accessorized, galaxy class babes more suited for a limo than a Prius Uber car. The ladies are each sporting sheik rose colored glasses. They almost looked like twins with their shades on. But the gals are from two different worlds. One works in online marketing/PR. The other was the client. I have no idea what business *she* was in, as the generic jargon they were using provided scant clues.

I found it fascinating that Marketing Girl had come up with such an out-of-the-box idea. What was she like? How smart would she come off if I could engage her in conversation? Alas, that was not to happen. Once ensconced in the car and off to

Bacara the women were locked in exclusive dialog. I was excluded from the conversation the entire way up to the resort. After one or two chime-ins early on it was clear that any further words coming from my mouth other than *"We're here"* would have been an intrusion. All I could offer was a safe comfortable ride. And that was just fine.

What actually was going on in the back seat was that Marketing Girl was *working* Client Girl. She was controlling the conversation, testing for weak spots in the client's business model that her firm could fill. Offering assistance when holes were found. Client Girl seemed fairly new to her position and did not appear thrilled with her "team." Marketing Girl had solutions for that dilemma too. The whole trip, was about firming up the rapport and bringing Client Girl under Marketing Girl's umbrella of services. Smoothly. She was a real professional.

At ride's end I swung into the open lobby portal at Bacara, announced *"We're here"*, and my fare exited the car. Client Girl gave me a short but warm thank you. There was no tip. The women had other things on their minds.

Uber Story   Uber Story   Uber Story

One Way to Pay for College

While in town one late night I get a pickup at the Spearmint Rhino Gentlemen's Club, a worldwide chain of strip clubs. I pull up to the club and scan for my fare. A doorman motions a woman to the car. Here she comes. Clearly it is one of the club strippers. She's dressed for it. The lady needs a ride home, which is somewhere in the student housing complex on the UCSB campus. She gets in the car. The doorman gives me a look like *"Uh huh, that's right pal."* I head to the freeway, pondering what kind of a ride this was going to be.

It turned out to be a singularly boring and uncomfortable ride. The girl is on the phone in a heartbeat. She sounded down, and was seeking solace from someone on the other end of the line. She announces to her friend that it hasn't been a good night. Her voice is full of melancholy.

Unfortunately I get on the freeway in the wrong direction, heading south away from the campus, instead of north. She caught the mistake before I did.

Stripper: "Sir? Where are you going? You're going the wrong way."

Uber James: "Oh you're right. I'm sorry. I'll exit and we'll turn around."

The next exit, Milpas Street, had **two** exits depending on which side of the freeway you wanted to end up on. I wanted to end up on the other side to take the northbound onramp, which was the second exit. As I passed the first exit I hear:

Stripper: "Sir? What are you doing?

Uber James: "I'm taking the second exit. It will take us to the northbound ramp quicker.

Stripper: (silence)

The tone of her voice telegraphed concern about my mistake. And after I briefly apologized (so as to not interrupt her call) *I* start to feel uncomfortable. It's not what she says, it's what she *doesn't* say. She doesn't do what people normally do at this juncture... which is to gesture in some way that the error was no big deal. She did not pay attention to that element. And not that *that* is a big deal, but it would have released the tension.

So we get on the freeway in the correct direction. The girl is still talking on the phone. Should something else be said? Should I tell her I'm sorry that I made her nervous? That it's late, it's dark, and I'm tired.

Was she afraid that she might be kidnapped, tied up, taken away, and held for ransom? Or have I just listened to that Tom Petty song one too many times? Fact is, the problem with explanations is that sometimes they make things worse. This would undoubtedly be one of those times.

I say nothing. We get closer to the university when suddenly the young lady wants to get off a couple of freeway exits early and hit a nearby In-N-Out burger. I pull into the parking lot. She gets off the phone and exits the car. I have no idea if she wants me to wait while she grabs a burger. She's not talkin'. So I ask her. No, she wants to end the trip. She will be staying at In-N-Out for a while.

So that was that. I had to ask myself if she ended the ride early because the Uber driver had startled her and she didn't want him to know where she lived... or did she just fancy a burger. My paranoid mind says the former. My logical mind says the latter. To settle the question (right now, as I'm writing this story) I'll just go with the back half of that song lyric: "*Honey, it don't really matter to me... Baby, you believe what you want to believe.*"

By the way in my short Uber career I had three pickups for UCSB students who were in some way working in the sex trade. Presumably to help pay for school. Nice work if you can get it.

Maybe.

Uber Story   🚗   Uber Story   🚗   Uber Story

Caught in a Catch-22

Santa Barbara is an expensive city to live in. Everyone wants to live in Santa Barbara. Your author lived there for a while. Clean air, afternoon ocean breezes, the towering mountains, the Pacific Ocean. The food, the shopping, the university. What's not to love?

If you work in Santa Barbara but can't afford to *live* in Santa Barbara, you commute from a surrounding community. If you don't have a car you might use Uber. If you are trying to save money to buy a car, but you're spending a big chunk of your salary on transportation to/from work... then you're in an endless loop. Such was the state a 20-something female was in when I gave her a ride to Summerland, a beachside bedroom community about fifteen minutes south of Santa Barbara. The young woman explained her quandary about not being able to save for a car. The dilemma seemed to be a dominant force in her life.

We had the time, so I threw a few options at her. One was that it was a great time to buy a car because many people who don't think they'd qualify for a loan in fact *would* qualify (auto loans had very relaxed lending standards at this time). Had she tried? (No). Then I told her about a car rental place near the airport called Rent-A-Wreck. She might be able to rent a car for less than her monthly Uber outlay.

She liked the ideas. Then there was some lamenting about how she wished her dad would offer such help, which he apparently wasn't. I let that one go. End of story.

Uber Story 🚗 Uber Story 🚗 Uber Story

The Woman Who Needed a New Friend

I get a ride request to pick up a woman at a residential address in an upper middleclass Santa Barbara neighborhood. I find the house and pull in the driveway. A 30ish looking woman appears after a bit and gets in the car. As sometimes happens there is a sad story regarding her need for an Uber ride, and in short order the story is revealed.

She asked me how I was doing, and I replied that I was having a good day. I asked her how *she* was doing and she replied *"I'm having the worse day of my life."* Uh oh. Caution, fragile package onboard. I respond with some words that open the door to her sharing the story, if she cared to. She walks through the door. *"I was driving down the freeway after just breaking up with my fiancé. I was crying my eyeballs out. Suddenly my car dies right on the freeway. Totally dead."*

The woman had managed to get the car over to the shoulder and dealt with getting it towed. Somehow she gets a ride over to her girlfriend's house, who is supposed to come home and help her out. The friend is a no-show. That's why the lady called for an Uber car. She goes on to tell me that her friend finally did call while the Uber car was on its way. The friend won't be able to get away for a while, but inquires as to what my fare will be doing later. My passenger tells her friend that she already has a dinner engagement.

On that note the girlfriend invites herself to the dinner. She takes a selfie, sends it to my fare, inquiring if she is dressed ok for dinner. That is the total extent of support rendered to her friend in distress.

Note: Uber James to "friend": Hello!? Just a third party observation here. You might want to take your head out of your Petunia patch for a moment and have a look at what's going on outside of yourself. Just a thought.

By now we arrived at my fare's house. Before she gets out I offer to wait till she has cleaned up and then take her to the restaurant at no charge. It seemed the gal was due for one nice gesture that day. She is touched by the offer but declines. She's going to get picked up. I wish her well and drive off.

Uber Story   🚗   Uber Story   🚗   Uber Story

College Kids Overwhelm the Uber Network

Here is a good example of why I preferred driving Uber in wine country over Santa Barbara. There's no huge party colleges. One night the Prius is summoned for a pickup at an apartment complex a few blocks from Santa Barbara City College. The college is several miles south from its big brother; UCSB (University of California at Santa Barbara). However, UCSB students are known to frequent the parties at City College because the authorities have cracked down on the notorious UCSB campus partying.

I come up on the apartment building and it's like something out of a summer break movie. The entire area in and around the complex is teeming with drunk people. They're as thick as ants. Every apartment in this sort of horseshoe shaped building is participating. People are staggering in and out of doorways. Others are milling about –and hanging over– the concrete walkways on both of the two floors. The courtyard is totally packed. People are spilling out onto the sidewalk and into the street. The cops are arriving.

It's pandemonium. And somehow Uber James has to find his fare in this cauldron of flesh. I try to call the fare. A young man answers but he is so high he cannot speak intelligibly. All I hear is some disembodied mumbling about how he has to get home. But no clue as to his whereabouts. GPS was about as helpful as a 10 year-old at a construction site. I tell him where I'm parked (right in front, in plain sight). The line suddenly goes dead. I try a couple of more times to reach him. No joy. I now realize that the situation has gone beyond any resemblance of rationality. The sea of drugged out humanity pushing out of the complex is too great.

So I take an action rarely employed and cancel the ride.

Immediately the app starts flashing with a new request. I accept the ride. It's from the same building. I cancel. The app lights up again for the same address. I ignore the request. I try and go **OFFLINE** because Uber tracks both ignored requests and cancelled rides in the driver's statistics. But I can't go **OFFLINE** because the requests are coming in back to back. I can't even turn off the phone because the car would still be seen by the Uber network as **ONLINE**. So, I ignore the phone, pick a heading that will take me as far away from the party as possible, and speed off. Ten minutes later the block party was another Uber driver's problem.

Sorry 'bout that.

Uber Story   🚗   Uber Story   🚗   Uber Story

Speaking of UCSB

Speaking of UCSB, if you drive for an on demand ride service like Lyft or Uber (Lyft is in SB but not in the Santa Ynez Valley) you *are* going to find yourself on campus quite often. People there are always wanting rides, either because they don't have a car (common), or because they are being responsible drinkers (common). Most pickups seem to come from Isla Vista, the off-campus township that houses thousands of students. But ride requests come from all across the UCSB landmass squeezed between the SB airport and the ocean. I've heard of drivers specializing in giving rides only at UCSB, and one guy in particular who installed a rotating disco ball in his car to entertain his passengers.

Daytime pickups are of course different from nighttime pickups. You get a broad range of students of course, but I was rather amazed at how many Asian nationals, in particular Chinese, got into the car on campus. Both Santa Barbara and UCSB have a number of language schools. This partially accounts for the rather large population of foreign students. But many Chinese are studying the same subjects as the Americans. When queried, my Chinese passengers often cited math as their major. It sounds stereotypical, but based upon my **very informal** survey (see the preface), math seems to rule among Asian students. Conversely I had a young Chinese girl claim she was weak at math but spoke four languages. Her mother had urged her to therefore play into her strength. So the student was here to learn yet another language.

I've had a lot of really smart and interesting students take Uber rides in the Prius. One ride that stands out was a young man who was studying Sound Engineering Management and Agricultural Economics. What a combo. His basic love was music, and that's where the sound engineering came in. But there was also a strong tug to *save the world*, although he didn't put it like that. That's where his interest in the economics of agriculture came in. He was a very aware, conscious, socially responsible person. And I 'm happy to report that he was not the only one of his ilk I had the honor to give a ride to. There are some very conscious young people out there. If you read the book "Generations" it hints that people of his [college] age group who will save the planet.

Uber Story   🚗   Uber Story   🚗   Uber Story

If You Love Her Then You Must ....

Where is Mama Cass and John Phillips of The Mamas and the Papas when you need an update to their hit 1966 song 'Words of Love'? The tune, written by Phillips and sung by Cass, made the case that *words* of love were no longer enough and that *actions* were now required to properly woo your love into marriage. The song recommends sending her *"somewhere where she's never been before."*

Skipping to present day, the thoroughly modern social media aware couple I picked up one night had turned the *Words of Love* theme on its head. Rather than send her on a trip the man had brought the trip to his girl. The boyfriend had flown in twenty-seven of his girlfriend's closest personal friends for an engagement party.

But I'm getting ahead of the story. Let's back up. It's nighttime.

The Uber app beckons me to the Funk Zone. Two very happy people find the car and hop in. They are well lubricated, but on top of that the captivating couple is sort of... glowing. Turns out that the gentleman had recently proposed marriage. And they wanted to tell me all about it as I was driving them to dinner. But first we had to stop by their hotel, which was actually a large but quaint B&B known as the 'Simpson House' which is ensconced in an unobtrusive, heavily wooded neighborhood near downtown. It was frightfully difficult to get in and out of the establishment as there is only one way in and out, no turn around, and the driveway is less than a lane wide. We park all the way at the end of the driveway and the girlfriend goes in to retrieve whatever it was she needed to retrieve. During the downtime the boyfriend shows me his buffed '55 Chevy. He had done the restoration himself and of course my flash-less nighttime snapshot does not do the car justice. It was a sweet looking automobile.

Pretty hard to see in the dark but this was one sweet 55
Chevy

But what was this SoCal couple doing in SB having an engagement party on the very weekend of the proposal? How does the
math on that one work? These things apparently do happen.
Don't forget that we ran into a similar story in chapter 12, 'The
Conspiracy'. Let's see how this particular scenario unfolded.

I fight the car out of the driveway and once in the street the
splainin' commences. The guy clarifies that he'd been planning the whole affair for six months. He had navigated a
logistical honeycomb, coordinating availability of nearly 30
people to drive and fly in from all over the country and book
into the B&B. So he not only orchestrated the entire event,
right down to a cover story as to why the couple was heading
up to Santa Barbara for the weekend, he has managed to
keep the whole thing a SECRET from his gal the entire
time.

This from a guy's guy who restores classic cars as a hobby. Not bad.

Now of course there's a giant unanswered question associated with this story: How did Boyfriend know that Girlfriend would say yes to the relationship upgrade? The answer is the same as in the other story... he *knew*.

Now we get the feminine perspective. Girlfriend tells me that she was indeed clueless the whole time. But she *did* get suspicious about the drive up to SB. The cover story was that they were going to a car show but she wasn't buying it. Still, even though she knew something was up she had no idea that a proposal and a deluxe B&B stuffed full of her friends awaited their arrival.

Clearly the woman was massively impressed about the trouble her guy had gone to. Happy juice or no happy juice this was one happy couple. I wish them the best.

And Now it's Time for Another Uber Poem

When noble citizens need a ride
and can't bear to give up their pride
when wasting cash they can't abide
there trusty app lets out a cry
for Uber-car... *Uber-car*
Uber-car... *Uber-car*
speed of lightning, roar of thunder
comes Uber-car, without a blunder
Uber-car. Uber-car!
when in this world the headlines read
that cabbies hearts are filled with greed
they overcharge all those in need
to right this wrong with blinding speed
goes Uber-car... *Uber-car*
Uber-car... *Uber-car*
speed of lightning, roar of thunder
comes Uber-car, without a blunder
Uber-car. Uber-car!

SIXTEEN
QUICKIES - 16 MINI UBER STORIES

"People are funny"
-Art Linkletter

1. A Cal Poly (California Polytechnic University) Electrical Engineering alumnus of one year gets in the car for an Uber ride. He speaks of having a great job, so I ask him why so many college grads these days are unemployed and stuck with ferocious student loan payments. His retort: *"They took the wrong major."*

2. A young couple gets in the car from a Solvang motel to go wine tasting. They had just had some kind of a scuffle and the man is sulking a bit. The woman offers that they had a rough start to their day but she told her man they were going tasting anyway. *"I told him we're just gonna have to wine it out."*

3. In the span of two days, three passengers who formerly lived in L.A. tell me they left SoCal due to traffic. One quit their job due to the 1.5 hour commute and moved to Palm Springs. The other two had similar stories.

4. A solo woman day-trips from Santa Barbara to Los Olivos for a spa afternoon. I get to take her back to SB. On the way she tells me she named her son after Stevie Wonder (the boy's middle name is Wonder). Sometime after having her baby she had attended a Stevie Wonder concert. She described walking backstage before the concert to try and see Stevie. She slipped past security and walked into his dressing room, and told him what she had named her child. Security rushed in, but Stevie called them off and let her stay. She relays to me that after they talked she asked him for a hug, and when Stevie complied, the

largess feeling of love emitting from the man was like nothing she had ever experienced.

5. One day I'm getting off the 101 freeway in Buellton. There is a stopped car blocking the exit ramp about 100 feet from the stop sign. I pull up on the shoulder next to the car to see what's up. It's a woman from Arkansas who had pulled off the freeway to call her mother back home (apparently blocking exit lanes is legal in Arkansas, if it's really important).

6. Three tipsy ladies who rarely drink wine get in the car and yell out: "*Step on it Uber James!*" They then giggle themselves silly at what they just said. (As mentioned in the introduction I had been fortunate to also get a "*Keep the meter running*" and a "*Follow that car.*" Made me feel like a real life cabbie.)

7. Four girls are in and out of the Prius for several rides throughout the day. One girl in particular is relegated to sitting in the front seat every ride. How is that determined? There's definitely a nonverbal pecking order invoked at such times. The front seat girl isn't as pretty as the other flowers in the garden. She's also a touch abrasive in her manner. Furthermore, she speaks at a higher volume than the other girls, and I get the impression it's not just because she's in front. It appears more her natural voice, compensating for being ignored over the years. She may or may not have been aware that speaking loudly had incurred the exact opposite effect, pushing her further from the clique.

8. *Overheard from the back seat*: A girl is chatting with her gal pal on the phone. Clearly she still lives at home. She says that she and her boyfriend each go to

bed with a skype call running on their smartphones so that they can hear each other sleeping.

9. I run into a couple in Los Olivos that had taken a ride earlier in the day. They are coming out of a tasting room that I happen to be parked in front of after dropping off a fare. We smile and say hello, and I notice the gentleman is burdened with wine bottles they are carrying from one tasting room to another. I offer to take the bottles in my car and drop them at their hotel later (this was a no-brainer for me and I didn't expect a tip because I drive by all these locations throughout the day). The couple exchanges a glance, the man stiffens a bit, and tells me no thanks, and that they may see me later when they Uber back to the hotel. Clearly the suggestion had weirded them out. Such an offer did not seem to compute by any social math the couple was aware of. I am impulsed to assure them this was not a covert move to steal their wine, but as with the stripper in Chapter 15, further conversation would have just reinforced the awkwardness of the moment. I smiled and said goodbye.

10. A really bright guy who used to work for Elon Musk (Tesla, SpaceX) on artificial intelligence gets into the car with his wife. I am taking them from Solvang to Santa Barbara. The temptation to query the man as to when he thinks AI will come into being is overwhelming. He guesses 50 years. We spend the bulk of the drive discussing AI, consciousness, intelligence, sentience, ghost in the machine, morality and whatnot. At the end of the ride I'm more convinced than ever we will not see *true* AI in our lifetimes. At least I certainly hope not.

11. I pick up a pilot at the Santa Barbara airport. He has just flown in from Reno in his private plane. He and his wife had attended a wedding in SB at the five-star Biltmore hotel earlier in the week. His wife wanted to stay and explore the area, so he flew home on his own to take care of some business. Now he has flown back to retrieve his wife. He was so used to flying it meant little to run home for a while and then retrieve the missus when she was ready. Gotta love that. (Parenthetically, this was in September. The pilot told me he could barely see Lake Tahoe when he flew over due to the smoke from all the fires.)

12. I have a conversation with a couple as to whether people are getting better looking. The consensus is yes.

13. An Australian tourist informs me that because of Uber's presence in Australia, cab 'medallions', which bestow the right to drive a taxi, had dropped in value from $300K to $60K, and even at the reduced price were difficult sell.

14. A pilot on his way to the Santa Ynez airport tells me that he has four Priuses of various vintages in his family, and the only repair needed to date was to replace the starter battery in one car. He tells me that all the taxis in Seattle have switched to the Prius. When I comment that the key must be to treat them well and they will treat you well... he informs me he drives his Prius *"like a go-kart."*

15. A couple from Europe currently working in America are getting married... in America. They are not going home to where the bulk of their family and friends are. When I inquire as to why, the couple whispers that it's a strategy to keep the number of attendees

down. Only the people who really want to be with them will go to the effort.

16. A young man takes an Uber ride while I'm in the Hollywood area after driving three Chinese tourists down from Solvang. We drive by a giant billboard advertising the latest Star Wars film; 'Rogue One'. We talk. He's seen it. I haven't. He's a huge-o fan. I'm a huge-o fan. I tell him that I'm old enough to have seen the premiere of 'A New Hope' in 1977 in San Francisco, and that I refuse to see a Star Wars film since George Lucas sold the franchise, due to the 'Disneyfication' factor. He sees my point, and was not crazy about The Force Awakens... but has gone back to see Rogue One five times that week. This gives me something to think about. When exiting the car he calls out: *"May the Force be with you."* Without delay I reply *"Live long and prosper."* He laughs.

SEVENTEEN
THE LAST CHAPTER

Uber James' Last Night

Leaving the Valley

Lessons Learned

"All's Well That Ends Well"
- Title of 1604 play by William Shakespeare

Uber James' Last Night

All the stories related in the prior chapters occurred between August 26th and November 6th, which was my last evening driving Uber before returning home. At that point California had experienced a couple of rainstorms and the fire in Big Sur was essentially out. I had stayed on in the valley a couple weeks past the all-clear signal in order to fulfill a few driving commitments. By now the tourists were in ever declining numbers, the bulge of wedding fares had subsided, so all things considered it was clear that my totally unexpected summer vacation had come to an end.

There were a few uneventful fares that last night. After delivering the passengers to their point B's I drove to my cherished El Rancho Market for a final post 7PM ½ price dinner from the deli. The clerk asks me how I'm doing and I tell him I'm ok, just having a little trouble coming off of daylights savings time. We had just set our clocks back, and the election was in two days. I tell him that the first Presidential candidate who promises to repeal daylights savings time gets my vote. We laugh.

Leaving the Valley

The following morning I packed up my gear, checked out of the motel, traded goodbyes with Johnny and his wife Jessie, and checked mail for the last time. The Uber signs promised for many months never did make an appearance. I then headed over to Caesar's Hand Car Wash. I had been washing the car every day while Ubering, and had learned at some point that the oh-so-convenient automatic car wash places were putting nasty swirl marks in the paint, so that habit had been discontinued. Fortunately there was a well-reputed hand car wash over in Santa Ynez called Caesar's Auto Detailing. Although Caesar's was slower and more expensive, the guys there took splendid care of the Prius. After the car wash, and a haircut, I pointed the car north and back to uncivilization. The odyssey was complete.

Lessons Learned

Driving Uber gives one insight to a cross section of our culture. The time spent driving fares from point A to point B was full of lessons. Here's a few that stuck in my mind. Keep in mind that some of these impressions are colored by having lived outside pop culture for 15 years.

- If you don't judge people they will love you.
- Driving can be used as a tool for personal growth.
- Selfishness –*you OR me thinking*- can be overcome. Just as darkness is simply the absence of light, and evil is simply the absence of good, pure self-interest is simply the absence of compassion for others. Awareness and willingness may be tools to transcend the visceral reaction to put yourself first- *i.e. you AND me thinking*.
- There are some beautiful souls occupying this planet.
- The state of automobile technology is such that current hybrid sedans allow for good fuel economy without compromise. To my surprise I found the Prius

to have power, comfort, roominess, cargo space, looks... and 50-60 MPG.

- It's impossible for an Uber driver to obtain a 5-star rating on every ride.
- People really like Starburst candies
- Everyone everywhere is looking DOWN. At their smartphones. I actually saw a woman crossing the street on a bicycle looking down at her phone the whole time.
- Nearly all the young adults who played their own music in the car seemed to be listening to either rap or Britney Spears knockoffs (I'm **sure** that dates me). I was surprised when some women were not offended by rap lyrics denigrating females.
- College students at UCSB and Cal Poly seem very racially integrated. Groups of many racial flavors piled into the car and were quite comfortable with each other. Conversely, races from countries with limited English skills, such as some Chinese, flocked with their own kind. Language, and perhaps culture, seemed the only dividers.
- When drinking, women sometimes have just as dirty mouths as men. Dirty as in how people talk in so many TV shows now, such as 'Silicon Valley'. There seems to be no place where 4-letter words are persona non grata these days. Even books titles appearing on G Rated Amazon now have the F word in the title. No censorship. Is art imitating life, or the reverse?
- People get along better when they make fun of each other's weaknesses and shortcomings. It lets the steam off. But it has to be agreed to by all in the group, either implicitly or explicitly. Otherwise feelings get hurt.

- Many people are run almost exclusively by fear in their daily lives.
- Bachelorette parties are multi-day affairs now. I did not have a single weekend *bachelor* party requesting a ride however.
- Who goes wine tasting? Couples, girls in groups, and gays. I never took a group of heterosexual males wine tasting.
- We're living in the future. The long anticipated "future" has arrived. It's not quite the Jetson's, but we're getting awful close. But we need to keep our house in order because if we don't it might be right back to the Flintstone's for us all.
- Human history is branded by a constant process of one group of people displacing another group of people... culturally, genetically, or geographically. The history of the Santa Ynez Valley right up to this very day exemplifies this assertion, as the Chumash people use their gaming wealth to expand their sphere of influence.
- Most importantly... don't wash your BRAND NEW CAR at an automatic car wash.

I'm afraid *this* ride has come to an end. Hope you enjoyed it. Going **OFFLINE** now.

Oh, Ok. One more silly uber poem to see us out...

Have car will travel says the uber man
Amidst the hostile cabbies it's a savage land
His fast car for hire heeds the Uber app
A soldier of fortune is a guy called uber man
uber man uber man... where do you roam?
uber man uber man... far far from home